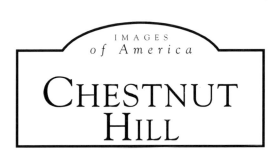

IMAGES
of America

CHESTNUT
HILL

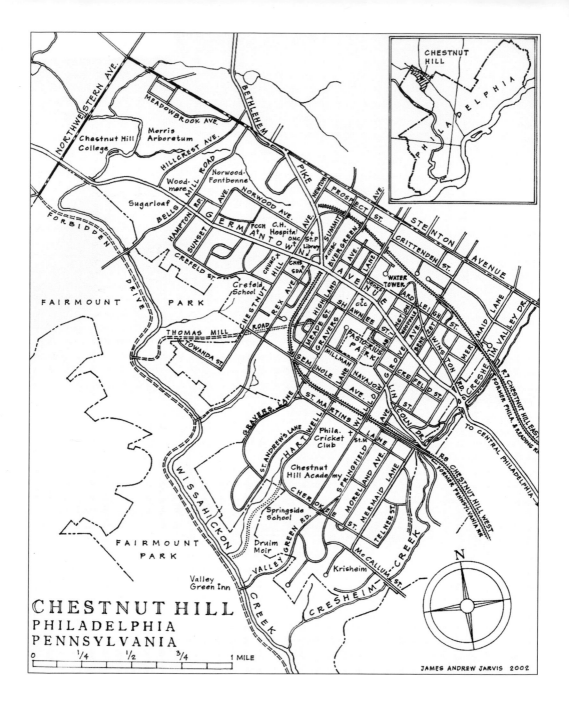

CHESTNUT HILL
PHILADELPHIA
PENNSYLVANIA

0   1/4   1/2   3/4   1 MILE

JAMES ANDREW JARVIS 2002

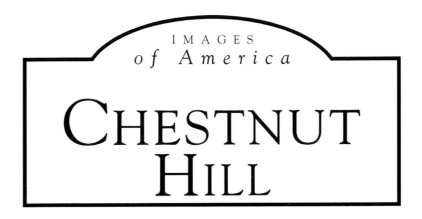

IMAGES
of America

CHESTNUT HILL

Thomas H. Keels and Elizabeth Farmer Jarvis for
the Chestnut Hill Historical Society

ARCADIA
PUBLISHING

Copyright © 2002 by the Chestnut Hill Historical Society
ISBN 978-0-7385-1061-3

Published by Arcadia Publishing
Charleston, South Carolina

Printed in the United States of America

Library of Congress Catalog Card Number: 2002106357

For all general information contact Arcadia Publishing at:
Telephone 843-853-2070
Fax 843-853-0044
E-mail sales@arcadiapublishing.com
For customer service and orders:
Toll-Free 1-888-313-2665

Visit us on the Internet at www.arcadiapublishing.com

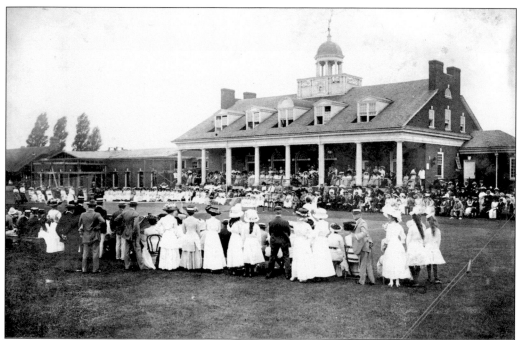

In 1887, the Philadelphia Cricket Club was the site of the first U.S. Lawn Tennis Championship for women. It moved to Forest Hills, New York, in 1922. This c. 1910 photograph may show a match from the women's singles championship. Richard Norris Williams II won the National Tennis Championship tournament at the Cricket Club in 1914 and 1916. Williams, a survivor of the sinking of the *Titanic* in 1912, won despite the terrible injuries he sustained after spending hours with his legs in the icy water. The Cricket Club clubhouse still stands, but without the cupola shown here. The ballroom is under construction on the left.

CONTENTS

ACKNOWLEDGMENTS

This book is a family photograph album for a community. Many Chestnut Hill residents contributed their ideas, expertise, recollections, and family photographs to make this book possible. Our thanks go to Chestnut Hill Historical Society executive director Peter Lapham and president John Levitties, who have supported the project wholeheartedly. We give our appreciation to staff members Audrey Simpson and Rosemary Lord as well as volunteer Susan Anthony for their support and hard work. Our reviewers contributed their extraordinary depth of knowledge about Chestnut Hill: Jefferson Moak, David Contosta, Emily Cooperman, Judith Callard, Linda Stanley, Janet Potter, and James Duffin made our work more accurate, informed, and readable. We are indebted to Christopher Lane and the Philadelphia Print Shop staff for allowing us to scan the photographs using their equipment.

Special thanks go to the Germantown Historical Society, our sister institution, for the lion's share of loaned photographs. Judith Callard and Mary Dabney graciously shared their experience gained producing a similar book for Arcadia, saving us much time and helping us improve our own efforts. Marion Rosenbaum, Irvin Miller, and Eugene Stackhouse aided us in mining the collection, without fees or restrictions, an example of historical societies supporting each other.

We are deeply indebted to the many institutions and individuals who allowed us to use their photographs and who are listed on page 128. This book would not have been possible without their assistance.

We greatly appreciate the generosity of those who gave photographs to the Chestnut Hill Historical Society, strengthening our growing collection. These donors are Justin M. and Nancy Dunning Baxter, Emilie Rivinus Bregy, Will Brown, Marianna Hagan, James H. Hill Jr., David Lockard, and the Philadelphia Cricket Club. We recognize others who contributed information and shared their knowledge: William Bassett, Elizabeth Shantz Bourquin, Sally Cornbrooks, Lester Escobedo, Elma G. Farnsworth, Alma Marcolina Fuess, William Gillies, Judy Goldschmidt, Patricia Gordon-Mann, Stewart Graham, Shirley Hanson, Joanne Grebe Hemberger, Peggy Hendrie, Naomi Colussi Houseal, John E. Jennings, Charles Lee, Jane Luddy, Dante Marcolina, Zilma Colussi Marcolina, Rudy Miles, Buddy Morasco, Carmen Notarianni, Kate O'Neill, Philip E. Pendleton, Phyllis Hunsberger Psichos, F. Markoe Rivinus, Gilda T. Roman, Joan Saverino, Evelyn Price Scott, Elizabeth Shellenberger, Samuel Smith, Edward Stainton, Gail Tomlinson, Barbara Tyson, Joseph Van Sciver, and Tony Wells. Photographer David J. Kerper worked hard to get the most out of old and sometimes faded and torn photographs. Robert DePue Brown gave his time to photograph 129 Bethlehem Pike. Judy and Anne Jarvis were diligent typists when their mother had a hand injury, and son Alex provided moral support.

We deeply thank the Bird in Hand Consignment Shop for its financial support. This publication would not have been possible without the generous funding of Quita Horan, who supported the historical society's efforts to gather information on early images of Chestnut Hill. Special thanks go to Larry Arrigale for his technical expertise, editing, proofreading, and infinite patience. Particular thanks go to an unsung hero, Andrew Jarvis, for his design and drawing of the Chestnut Hill map, locating the sites of unidentified photographs, fieldwork, writing, editing, and his unwavering support.

INTRODUCTION

As early as 1704, the name Chestnut Hill was given to a tiny village at the intersection of Germantown Pike and Bethlehem Pike in the northwestern corner of Philadelphia County. It is possible that the name derived from the many chestnut trees that encircled the hamlet. Eventually, Chestnut Hill spread over two of the original four land divisions of the German Township marked out by Francis Daniel Pastorius and the other founders in 1683—Sommerhausen and Crefeld, plus a small portion of Cresheim (present-day Mount Airy.)

By the Revolutionary War, Chestnut Hill had become a gateway village, linking Philadelphia with the rich interior farmlands of Pennsylvania. Farmers traveling to the city to sell their goods would stay at one of the many hotels lining Germantown Avenue, such as Cress's, Donat's, or the Mermaid. Gristmills and paper mills dotted the nearby Wissahickon and Cresheim Creeks and their tributaries. The rough-and-tumble village of millers and farmers, its main street lined with inns and taverns, did not have its first church building until 1822. In the opinion of an early Baptist minister, this was due to the "intense wickedness of the early inhabitants."

In 1854, two events changed the future of Chestnut Hill—the Chestnut Hill Railroad was opened from Germantown to Chestnut Hill, and the Act of Consolidation made Chestnut Hill part of the city of Philadelphia. Physically and politically, the rural village was now connected to the city. Soon, Chestnut Hill's healthy atmosphere and bucolic setting made it a favorite summer resort for Philadelphia's wealthy. Early developers such as Samuel Austin and Charles Taylor built summer houses on Summit Street, Norwood Avenue, and other streets near the Bethlehem Pike rail terminus. When service improved, Chestnut Hill became a year-round railroad suburb, the way Germantown had become a generation before.

In 1884, the Pennsylvania Railroad constructed a second line from Philadelphia through the west side of Chestnut Hill. Henry H. Houston, long associated with the "Pennsy," persuaded the railroad to build the line. Eventually, Houston would buy nearly 3,000 acres of land in Chestnut Hill and surrounding areas. From 1884 through 1895, he created a planned community named Wissahickon Heights. Dominated by Houston's own mansion, Druim Moir, Wissahickon Heights (later St. Martin's) had its own train station, social and recreational complexes (the Wissahickon Inn, Philadelphia Cricket Club, and the Philadelphia Horse Show), schools (Chestnut Hill Academy and Wissahickon Heights School), and church (St. Martin-in-the-Fields).

Between 1904 and 1935, Houston's daughter and son-in-law, Gertrude and George Woodward, and Houston's son Samuel, continued to develop the area, creating a series of influential residential complexes such as the French Village, Cotswold Village, and Tohopeka Court. Several are clustered around Pastorius Park, an English-style green developed by the Woodwards. Hoping to make Chestnut Hill a creative center, the Woodwards encouraged such disparate personalities as the Cogslea artists (Jessie Willcox Smith, Elizabeth Shippen Green, and Violet Oakley), conductor Leopold Stokowski, and the Willet Stained Glass Studio to move to the area. The Houstons and Woodwards rented most of their houses and carefully screened potential tenants, creating a social homogeneity that marked Chestnut Hill for many years.

Living side-by-side with the affluent was an active working neighborhood of shops and businesses. The Hill's bustling African-, Italian-, Irish-, and German-American communities were centered on the east side of Germantown Avenue. Italian-Americans, in particular, played a major role in Chestnut Hill's development. From 1880 through 1920, hundreds of Italians immigrated to Chestnut Hill to work primarily in quarries and stonemasons' yards. These new arrivals brought their distinctive cultures to Chestnut Hill, even forming separate social clubs for Northern Italians (the Venetian Club) and Southern Italians (the Bocce Club).

After World War II, Chestnut Hill wrestled with the problems of reduced municipal services, rising taxes, the breakup and development of large estates, and suburban flight. By the early 1950s, nearly 30 percent of all Germantown Avenue storefronts were vacant. Business leaders, including Lloyd Wells and J. Pennington Straus, reinvented Germantown Avenue as a "horizontal department store" by planting trees, erecting "colonial" façades, developing community parking lots, and mounting a cooperative advertising campaign. Today, the Chestnut Hill Business Association works to maintain Chestnut Hill's busy and attractive commercial district.

During the 1950s and 1960s, Chestnut Hillers also created many quasi governmental civic groups that revived the neighborhood while preserving its historic character, such as the Chestnut Hill Community Association, *Chestnut Hill Local*, and Chestnut Hill Historical Society. These organizations still act as local forums to shape policy on crime, social services, aesthetics, and other key issues. The Chestnut Hill Historical Society, working with the Friends of the Wissahickon, has developed a nationally recognized easement program for the preservation of open space and the protection of historic structures.

A National Historic District since 1985, Chestnut Hill is being considered for designation as a National Historic Landmark. Its architectural heritage ranges from colonial farmhouses to the Vanna Venturi House, Robert Venturi's 1964 classic of postmodern design. Because of its prominence as a railroad suburb, Chestnut Hill is especially rich in architecture of the 19th and early 20th centuries, with structures by John Notman, Thomas Ustick Walter, Frank Furness, Wilson Eyre, G.W. & W.D. Hewitt, Horace Trumbauer, Mellor Meigs & Howe, Robert McGoodwin, and Edmund B. Gilchrist. Besides Venturi, Chestnut Hill also features buildings by such modern masters as Louis Kahn, Oscar Stonorov, and Romaldo Giurgola.

Today, Chestnut Hill is one of the most vibrant and attractive neighborhoods in Philadelphia. Its restaurants and shops, along with its seasonal festivals, attract visitors from around the region. Chestnut Hill boasts such cultural attractions as the Morris Arboretum of the University of Pennsylvania, the Woodmere Art Museum, and the Philadelphia Bach Festival. Bordered on the southwest by the Wissahickon Valley section of Fairmount Park, Chestnut Hill is filled with other green spaces such as the Andorra Natural Area and Pastorius Park. Given its tree-lined streets and lush private gardens, it is not surprising that Chestnut Hill has been named Philadelphia's official Garden District. To the many people who live, work, or visit here, Chestnut Hill remains a unique and special place.

One

THE GATEWAY VILLAGE

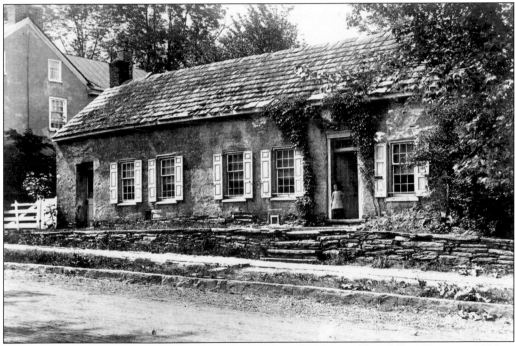

Chestnut Hill was originally part of the German Township granted by William Penn in 1683 to 13 Protestant families from Holland and what is now Germany seeking religious freedom and economic success. Present-day Chestnut Hill includes the areas once called Sommerhausen, Crefeld, and parts of Cresheim that were strung along Germantown Avenue. This major rural artery had few cross streets, unlike the grid system of Center City Philadelphia. The earliest recorded mention of the name Chestnut Hill is on a deed from 1704. As late as 1790, there were only 100 families in Sommerhausen, from Mermaid Lane to just below what is now Chestnut Hill Avenue. Daniel Snyder (born 1779) lived in this 18th-century house at the southwest corner of Germantown and Chestnut Hill Avenues.

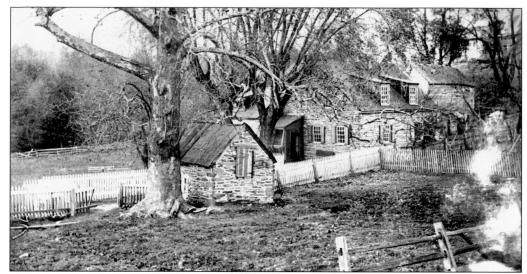

The area around Cresheim Creek attracted many early settlers, with about 12 houses built there by 1700. The Milan house, pictured here between 1900 and 1910, was located south of the Cresheim Creek between the present-day Chestnut Hill West railroad line and Cresheim Road. Hans Milan was the first owner of the Wyck house in Germantown. His son Matthias Milan acquired 100 acres of land in Cresheim and, by 1700, had built this two-story house, characteristic of many 18th-century farmsteads. The house was demolished in the 1920s. (Courtesy Germantown Historical Society.)

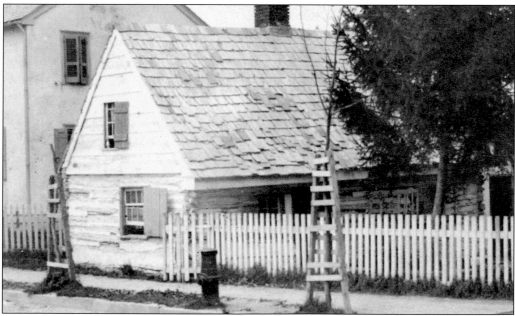

In 1759, Derrick Keyser, a carpenter, bought this log house (built 1743) with five acres. It once stood at the northeast corner of Germantown Avenue and Mermaid Lane. Sturdily built with hand-hewn logs notched together at the corners, it featured hand-split wood roof shingles. Windows then were typically small and few, and this house had one shutter per window. This photograph was probably taken in the 1880s, when the house was already more than 100 years old and when Germantown Avenue was still unpaved.

The John Rex house, now gone, was located at 8121–23 Germantown Avenue, on the east side, between Hartwell Lane and Abington Avenue, and was probably built between 1750 and 1770. Its central chimney and steep roof, which contained a two-story attic, were typical of houses built by Germanic settlers. Attics were used to store grain and supplies. These houses often had projecting second-floor joists supporting a pent roof. When these pent roofs rotted, as in this 1911 photograph, they often were not replaced. The porch is a later addition.

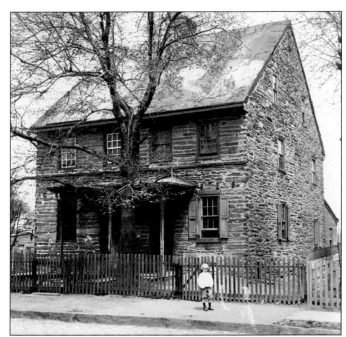

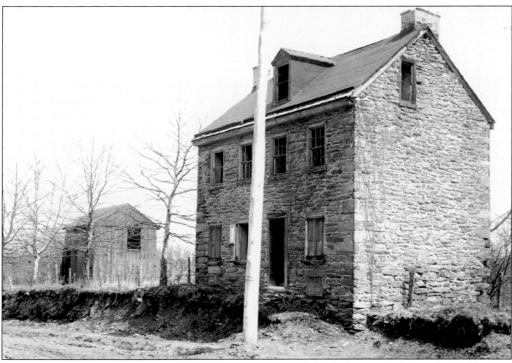

This house, located on Mermaid Lane west of St. Martin's Lane, is shown in 1913. The chimneys on the end walls and the shallower roof slope with dormer window are typical of 18th-century houses of English origin. By the end of the 18th century, the unifying feature of Chestnut Hill houses was the use of local stone for exterior walls. Wissahickon schist, also called Chestnut Hill stone, lay two to six feet under the soil of most of Chestnut Hill and was an excellent building material. (Courtesy Germantown Historical Society.)

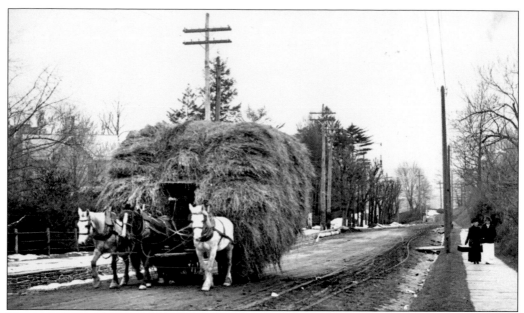

Three horses strain to pull a hay wagon up Bethlehem Pike in the early 1900s, a common scene for more than 150 years. Farmers from as far away as Reading and Bethlehem hauled their produce along Germantown Avenue and Bethlehem Pike to Philadelphia. Farmers often did not make the arduous trip all the way into Philadelphia but sold their goods at Chestnut Hill stores, where they could replenish their stocks of such necessities as salt, seeds, and dry goods. Merchants from Philadelphia would make the 10-mile trip to Chestnut Hill to purchase the produce for sale in the city.

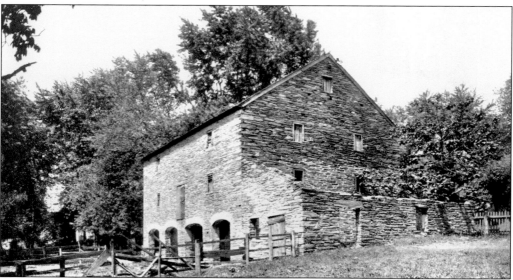

Abraham Rex, the brother of John Rex (see page 11), operated what was called a "great store" at what is now the Woodward company offices at 8031 Germantown Avenue. This barn behind the store was demolished to make way for houses on the north side of the first block of Wooddale Avenue (also known as Woodale Road). This view of the barn looks west from Wooddale Avenue toward Germantown Avenue. A date stone on the barn read, "J. & M. R. 1814," for John and Margaret Rex. John was the son of Abraham.

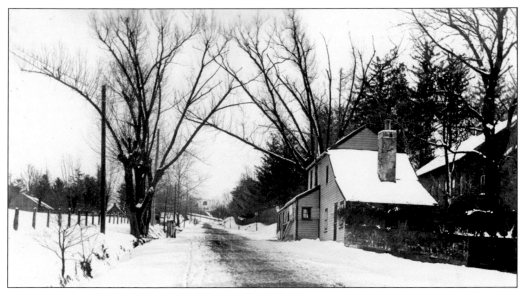

Bethlehem Pike and Germantown Avenue became toll roads in the early 19th century. Germantown Avenue was also called the Plymouth Road, Perkiomen Turnpike, or Reading Pike, as the road extended to those towns. Shown here in 1904 is the tollhouse on Bethlehem Pike. The tollgate is in the up position on the left side of the road. The tollhouse was located along present-day Stenton Avenue, just above Bell's Mill Road. Bethlehem Pike became a free road in 1904, and the tollhouse vanished by 1910. (Courtesy Germantown Historical Society.)

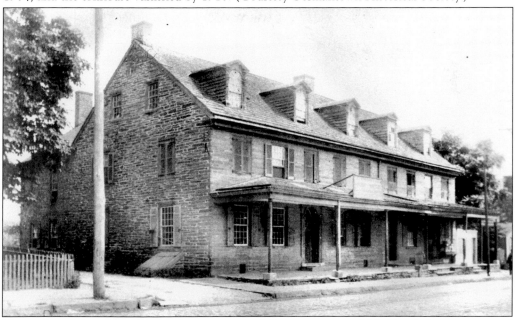

Henry Cress's hotel, at the northeast corner of Germantown and Highland Avenues, served stagecoach travelers; others served farmers. During the Revolutionary War, American soldiers used the hotel as a hospital, before it was burned by British troops in 1777. Rebuilt in the 1790s, the building was used as a refuge for Philadelphians from the yellow fever epidemic. This photograph was taken in 1904 before Highland Avenue was widened and the southern end of the building was removed, leaving four dormers.

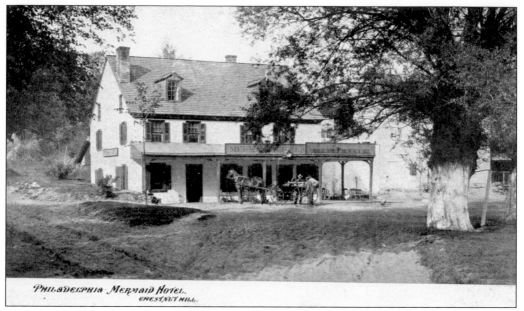

The Mermaid Hotel is believed to have been built in 1734. It was demolished to allow for the creation of Winston Road in 1913, and a new building was constructed. The Chestnut Hill Baptist Church used a pool behind the hotel for baptisms in the winter, when reaching the Wissahickon Creek was a hardship.

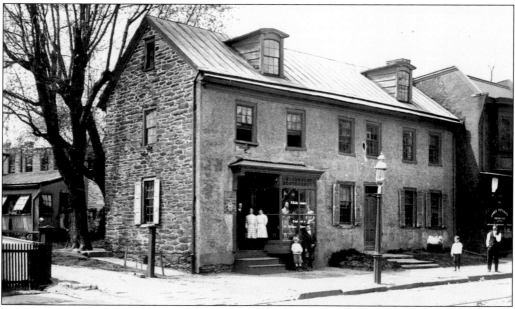

These two adjoining houses at 8132–34 Germantown Avenue were built before the Revolutionary War. Peter Kock owned the property in 1748, when a Swedish visitor wrote about his farm, "Every countryman . . . has commonly an orchard near his home. . . . We could scarcely walk in the orchard, without treading upon those peaches which had fallen off. . . . Only part of them were sold in town. . . . Everyone that passed by was at liberty to go into the orchard. . . . This fine fruit was frequently given to the swine." The houses were photographed in 1911. (Courtesy Germantown Historical Society.)

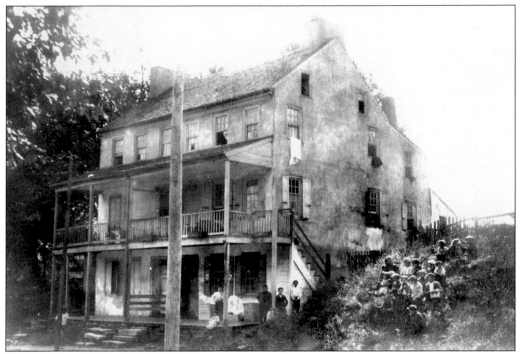

This house once stood at 7728 Germantown Avenue (above), on the west side, between Moreland and Springfield Avenues. Neighborhood children turned out below the sheet drying in the window for this 1904 photograph. Just above this house is 7718 Germantown Avenue, a narrow, two-bay house (below). These houses were on a large tract of land bought by John Roop in 1720. The tract extended from Germantown Avenue to the Roxborough line, bordered by what is now Mermaid Lane and Moreland Avenue. In 1887, Henry H. Houston bought most of the property on this block, and in 1923, the block was still part of the Houston estate.

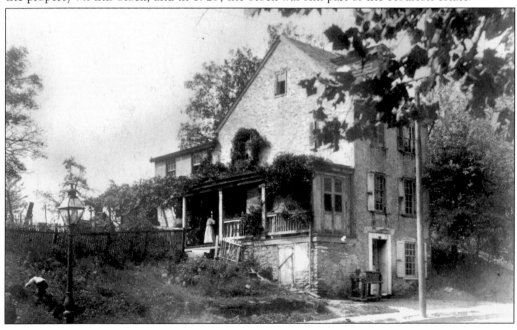

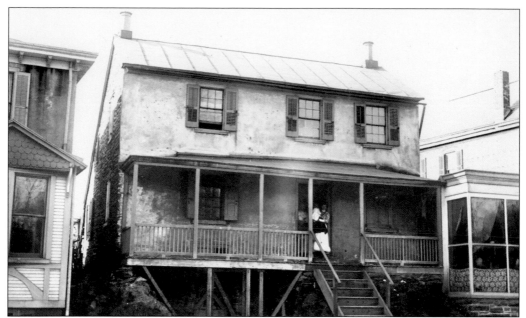

Town lots were laid out early in Chestnut Hill's development. In 1746, Bernard Kepler subdivided his farm into 10 one-acre parcels fronting on Germantown Avenue. He kept an "Avenue" between two of the parcels to maintain access to his farmhouse behind. This house stood at 8002 Germantown Avenue. The building, pictured here in 1911, was replaced in 1928 with a one-story commercial building now housing the Chestnut Hill Paint store. (Courtesy Germantown Historical Society.)

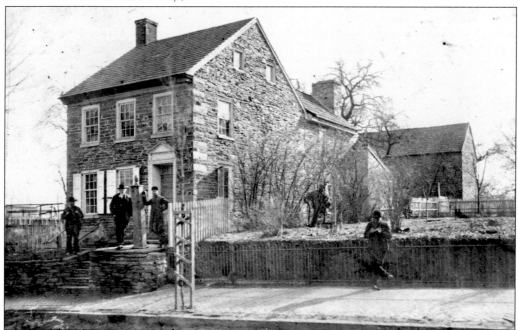

David Haas, with his son and grandson (both named Edward), pose in front of their Federal-style house in the 1880s. The farmhouse, with stone quoins at the corners and water pump out front, once stood at the southwest corner of Germantown Avenue and West Gravers Lane.

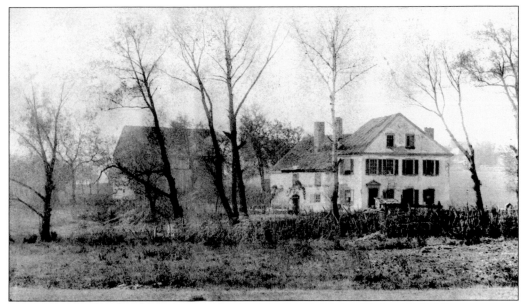

German immigrants Julius and Catherine Kerper purchased this land in 1765. Theirs was one of the most prosperous farms in Chestnut Hill. The Kerpers suffered great losses when British troops stormed through Chestnut Hill in December 1777, burning houses and taking goods. Hessian soldiers seized and later released Kerper's 14-year-old son Jacob, who was out checking his muskrat traps. Kerper rebuilt his destroyed house and sold it in 1795. The new owners built this Federal-style house abutting the earlier 18th-century house to the rear. The house survived until a fire in 1915, and the ruins were demolished to make way for Pastorius Park.

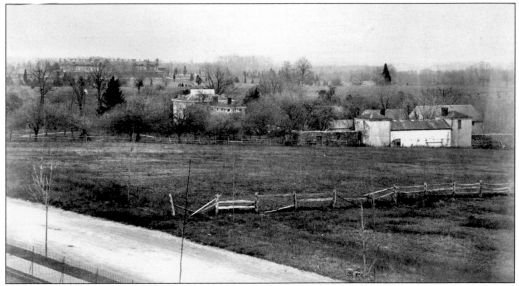

This c. 1886 photograph of the west side of the 8500 block of Seminole Avenue gives a glimpse into the rural past of Chestnut Hill. The building to the right was a silk manufactory, a remnant of the popular yet unsuccessful effort to grow mulberry trees and raise silkworms in the 1830s. A wood-plank sidewalk runs beside the dirt road. To the west are pastures leading down toward the Wissahickon. To the left is Boxly, the Frederick W. Taylor estate, with the rooftops of the Wissahickon Inn beyond.

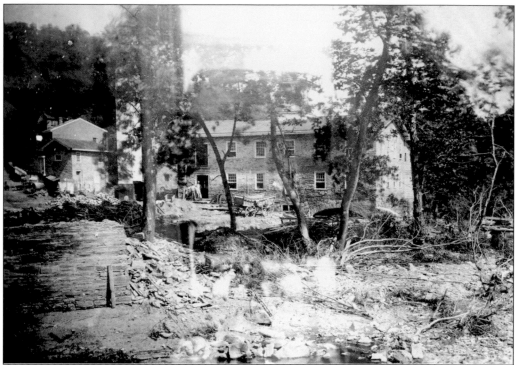

The many mills that lined the Wissahickon and Cresheim Creeks drew on outlying farms to obtain raw materials for processing. Grain was ground into flour for the markets of Philadelphia and shipped nationally and across the Atlantic Ocean. A gristmill was built in 1717 to the left of this site, later called the Thomas, Spruce, or Hanwell Mill. Edward Megargee, the proprietor, stands at the door of his mill, with a large Conestoga wagon out front. He purchased the mill in 1859, converting it into a paper mill. An arch spans the millrace, channeling the water that powers the mill. This mill was located on the east bank of the Wissahickon, just below the Thomas Mill covered bridge. (Courtesy Germantown Historical Society.)

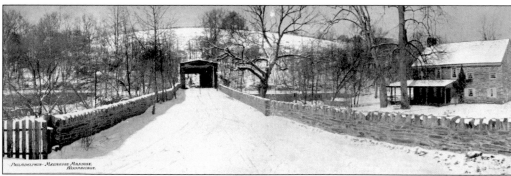

Thomas Mill Road, also called Spruce Mill Road, formerly began at Highland Avenue a bit west of Germantown Avenue, and cut a diagonal path northwest to the Wissahickon Creek. It was one of the few cross streets in Chestnut Hill in the 1700s. It exists now only from present-day Chestnut Hill Avenue to the Creek. The Fairmount Park Commission restored this covered bridge in 1939. The Barge house, pictured here, was built in 1803 and survived into the 20th century. It is now gone, and thick underbrush gives no hint of its existence. (Courtesy Germantown Historical Society.)

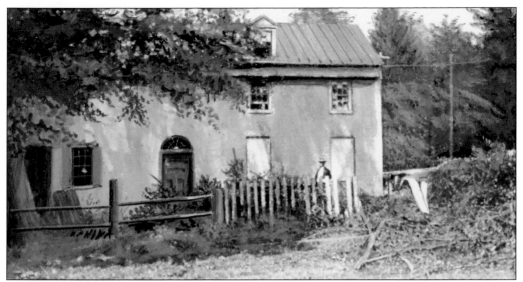

William Dewees, a native of Holland, was apprenticed to William Rittenhouse *c*. 1690 to learn to make paper from linen rags. In 1710, he built the second paper mill in America, at what was then called Crefeld, now the southern end of the grounds of Chestnut Hill College. His house, modified later in the 18th century, was on the west side of the Wissahickon where Harper's Meadow is today. The first congregation in Chestnut Hill met here, as no church building existed until 1822. They continued to hold their Reformed services there for 43 years. This Dewees house was used as a day school by the Sisters of St. Joseph and, in the 1890s, was demolished to make way for Fairmount Park. (Courtesy Germantown Historical Society.)

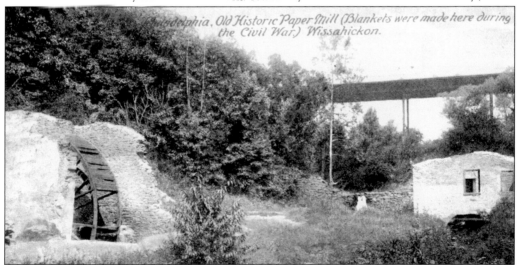

These are the ruins of the Patterson-Hill Mill with the mill wheel on the left and the Gorgas Fulling Mill with the stone arch visible at the bottom on the right. Both were along Cresheim Creek. A milldam may be seen in the center rear, and the McCallum Street Bridge in the background. Between 1725 and 1741, John Gorgas Sr. built a fulling mill for removing oil and grease from raw wool. A cotton mill was located on the other side of the creek in the mid-1800s. Millers dammed the Cresheim Creek in several places to create millponds, from which water would flow in a walled ditch, or race, to the mill building to turn the mill wheel to create power. The Houston family later purchased this area and deeded it to Fairmount Park.

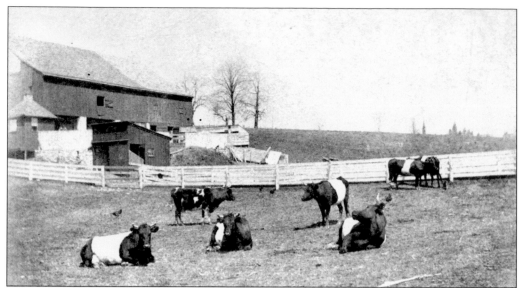

Hartwell Farm was bounded by Hartwell Lane, West Willow Grove Avenue, and Cherokee Street in the second half of the 19th century. Hiram Hartwell, a Center City grocer and hotel owner, bought this land to escape the city for the sake of his health. His farmhouse (603 West Hartwell Lane) and his barn (600 St. Andrews Road) still exists as residences. Railroad magnate Henry H. Houston bought this farm in 1886 and built his palatial home Druim Moir there. Part of his property was still a working farm in June 1894, when this photograph was taken. (Courtesy Germantown Historical Society.)

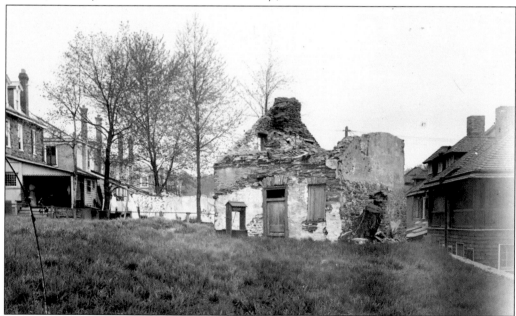

This early one-and-one-half-story house, built c. 1765, stood south of 7945 Germantown Avenue, midway between East Willow Grove Avenue and Benezet Street. Blacksmith Wigard Miller (died 1795) once owned this house. In the 1880s, it was used as a barn. An old stone path from Germantown Avenue leads to the site of house. This house originally stood alone, facing Germantown Avenue, flanked by fields and woods. (Courtesy Germantown Historical Society.)

Two

THE RAILROAD SUBURB

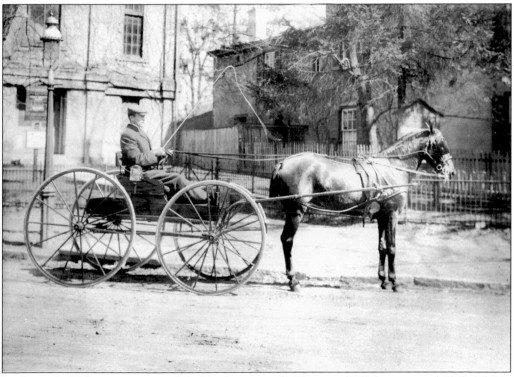

In the early 19th century, it took half a day to reach Chestnut Hill from central Philadelphia by carriage. The 10-mile journey was far enough to separate Chestnut Hill from the city and preserve its rural village character. Even before the railroad extended to Chestnut Hill in 1854, affluent Philadelphians were beginning to journey there as a summer destination. The advent of the railroads and trolley lines made the trip faster and, with improvements to Germantown Avenue, opened Chestnut Hill for suburban development. In 1854, the City of Philadelphia consolidated many outlying villages, including Chestnut Hill, within its new boundaries. This carriage waits outside the Chestnut Hill Baptist Church at the top of the hill.

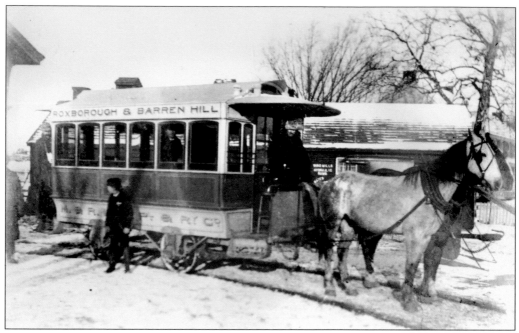

Before trolley cars were powered by overhead electrified lines, horses pulled horsecars like this one on rails. Beginning in 1859, horsecars shared the rails of the Germantown Passenger Railroad, which ran from Center City along Germantown Avenue to the horsecar depot at Westview Street, one mile south of Cresheim Creek. Riders to Chestnut Hill had to walk the rest of the way or arrange to be met by a horse and carriage.

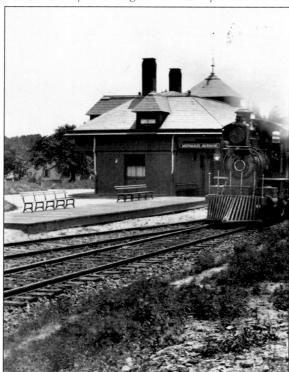

In 1847, a group of Chestnut Hill men began raising funds to build a railroad from Germantown to Chestnut Hill. The new rail line began operation in 1854 as far as Gravers Lane and was immediately successful. Four times a day, an engine pushed the cars up the hill, from which they returned by gravity. Riders changed trains in Germantown to go into Center City. Architect Frank Furness designed this station, built c. 1885 at the northeast corner of Mermaid Lane and the Reading tracks. It was demolished in the early 1930s. (Courtesy Germantown Historical Society.)

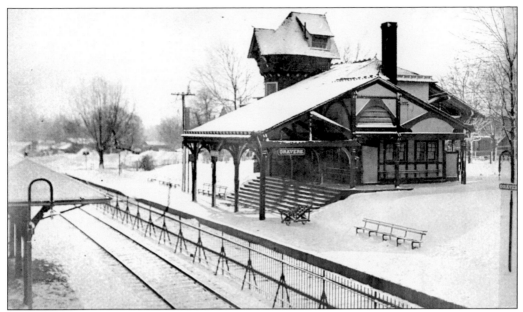

In 1870, the Chestnut Hill Railroad was leased to the Philadelphia and Reading Railroad. In the centennial year of 1876, there were 26 trains a day from Chestnut Hill. In 1884, the Pennsylvania Railroad opened a competing line to the west side of Chestnut Hill. The Reading decided to upgrade its stations in response to the competition. Gravers Lane station, designed by Frank Furness, was built in 1883. The Chestnut Hill Historical Society led its restoration in 1981, and it stands today.

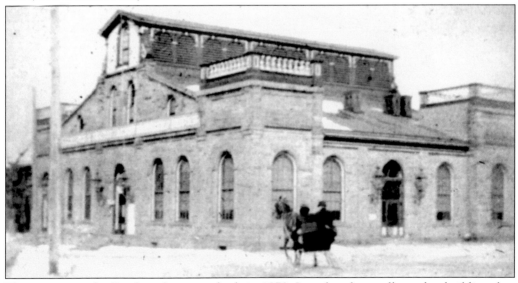

This station at the Reading depot was built in 1872. It replaced a small wooden building that served as the first depot. The upstairs hall became Chestnut Hill's first community center. To the north of the tracks on Bethlehem Pike was the Railroad House, an old farmhouse-turned-hotel for coachmen, who stabled their horses in the large stable behind. It was torn down in the late 1880s to make way for the roundhouse where steam engines were serviced. The station and roundhouse were demolished after the Reading line was electrified in 1930. The Chestnut Hill East station stands here now.

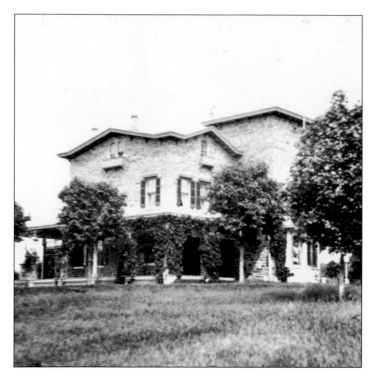

Publisher and lithographer Cephas G. Childs was elected to the board of managers of the Chestnut Hill Railroad in 1852. The new rail line increased property values in Chestnut Hill. Childs owned land at various times on Germantown Avenue, Bell's Mill Road, Prospect Avenue, and Bethlehem Pike. He owned this property from 1854 to 1855. This area was called Pumpkinville in 1840 and later Mechanicstown. This house, pictured in 1866, is now the Woodmere Art Museum and has been enlarged several times.

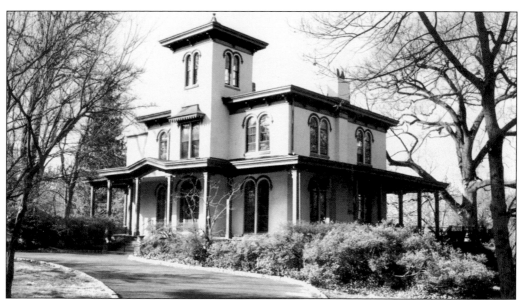

The Italianate style of architecture, with its observation towers, eave brackets, and half-round windows, was popular in the 1850s and 1860s in north Chestnut Hill. John Piper built this house, Pleasant View, in 1854, possibly on the site of another house. It was modeled after "The Italian Villa," by architect Samuel Sloan in his 1852 architectural treatise, *The Model Architect*. A newspaper advertisement for the sale of a property below the Chestnut Hill Railroad station on Bethlehem Pike read, "Beautiful situation, and for pleasantness and convenience and health is seldom surpassed."

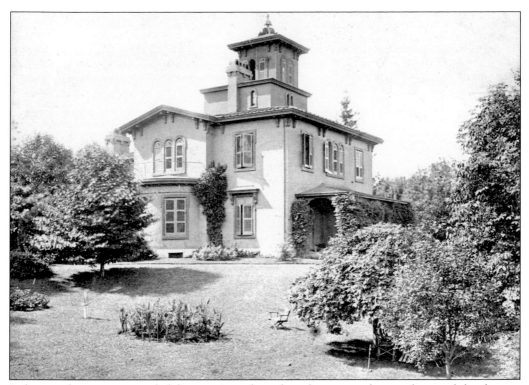

Italianate houses surrounded by manicured gardens began to change the rural landscape. Cephas Childs built this house *c.* 1850. Inglewood, at 154 Bethlehem Pike, exists today, but its appearance was completely altered by architects Cope and Stewardson in a Georgian Revival style in 1891. Only the rounded top windows on the north side give it away. In 1891, its owner, John Story Jenks, began to use this house as a summer residence, his primary residence being on Arch Street in Philadelphia.

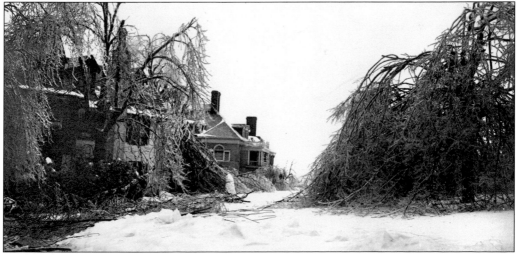

Inglewood is seen here in February 1902 after an ice storm rendered Chestnut Hill's roads impassable. Cephas Childs also built Inglewood Cottage (barely visible through the trees on the left) in 1850. It was designed by Thomas Ustick Walter, who also designed Girard College and the dome of the U.S. Capitol building.

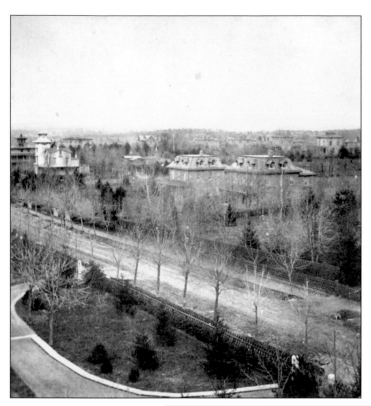

In 1854, Samuel Austin opened one of the earliest planned suburban streets, complete with sidewalks, at the highest elevation in Philadelphia, and called it Summit Street. It is pictured here in 1866. Until that time, every road in Chestnut Hill served a working purpose, such as access to mills or farm roads leading to the main thoroughfares. This stereopticon photograph was taken from 25 Summit Street, looking southeast toward Wyndmoor. One can see the identical houses at 42 and 46 Summit Street. Toward the left is 100 Summit Street, with its four-story tower, and the Evergreens house, which is now gone.

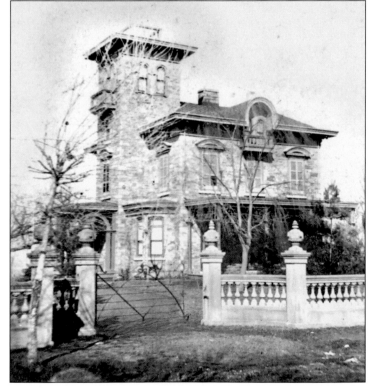

This house, at 17 Summit Street, was built near the actual summit in 1861 for Norman Hart, a hardware merchant. Its four-story tower, from which one could see miles out into the Whitemarsh Valley, was removed in 1948. The massive balustraded fence with urns, pictured here in 1866, was later replaced with a cast-iron fence. Many of the new Chestnut Hillers bought houses as second homes for the warm-weather months, retaining their Center City townhouses for the winter season.

When 32 Summit Street was built in 1859 or 1860, the windows on the third floor were circular. After this 1866 photograph was taken, these windows were enlarged to rectangles, which now extend to the roofline between the brackets. A balustrade surmounted the original first-story portico. In keeping with the contemporary ideal of a suburban home, John Naglee, a lumber merchant, laid out this manicured garden with shrubs, urns, and paths.

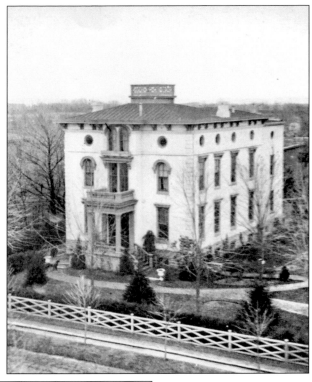

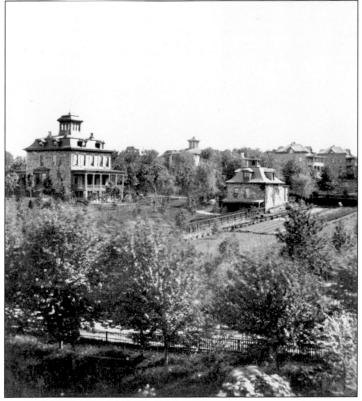

Two sets of granite posts, engraved with the initials RL, today mark the driveways of the Richard Levick house and carriage house at the northeast corner of Summit Street and Prospect Avenue, pictured here in 1866. The shoe merchant built his house in 1861, with a tower providing a commanding view of the farmland of Montgomery County. Stenton Avenue is in the foreground. The carriage house, with cupola, sits beside a large vegetable garden. The tower of 57 Summit Street, still there today, is visible in the center.

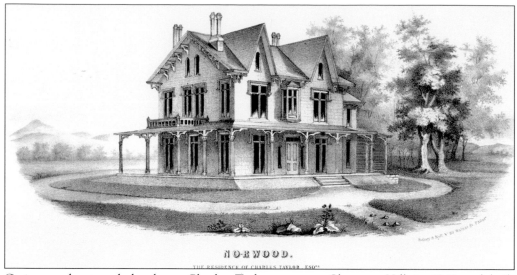

NORWOOD.

THE RESIDENCE OF CHARLES TAYLOR, ESQ.

Grain merchant and developer Charles Taylor came to Chestnut Hill in 1849 and built Norwood. The house was designed by the firm of Sidney and Neff, which designed several houses on Summit Street and Chestnut Hill Avenue. James C. Sidney, architect and civil engineer, surveyed and supervised construction of the Chestnut Hill Railroad bed. This image is a plate from his book *American Cottage and Villa Architecture*, published in 1850. Harriet Benson later used it as a summer residence, greatly altering its appearance with additions and a mansard roof. Today the building at 8891 Germantown Avenue is part of Norwood-Fontbonne Academy.

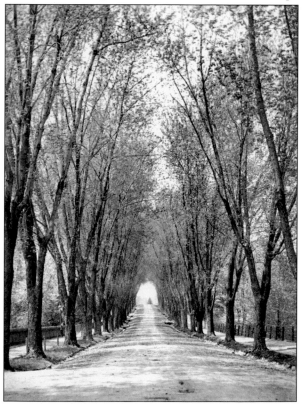

After accumulating about 40 acres in Chestnut Hill, Charles Taylor opened this road, Norwood Avenue, behind his house in 1860. To either side of this allée of elm trees he sold lots and built houses. The trees were fully grown by 1900, when this photograph was taken.

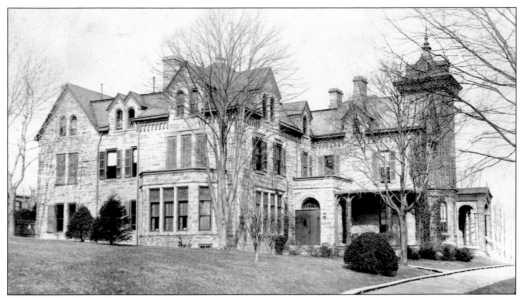

Charles Taylor built Edgecumbe at 8860 Norwood Avenue between 1862 and 1864, following a design resembling the published plans of architect Samuel Sloan. Arthur Howell, a leather goods merchant, lived there until 1876, when Charles B. Dunn, a banker, bought it. He enlarged it greatly, beginning in 1881, with architect Theophilus P. Chandler. Chandler returned in 1916, added to the south side, and removed the original Italianate tower on the north side.

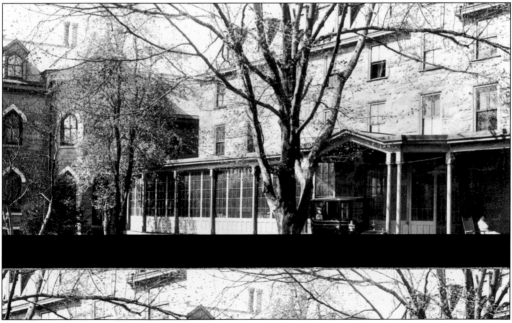

The Eldon Hotel, located at the southwest corner of Bethlehem Pike and Stenton Avenue and built c. 1860 as a private home, was one of three resort hotels in Chestnut Hill. In 1884, George Simpson built a second building (on the right) beside the original house. Just down the hill from the terminus of the Chestnut Hill Railroad line, the hotel served a growing number of wealthy Philadelphians from Center City. The Eldon operated as a hotel until 1910, when it was converted into the Kenwood mental sanatorium, pictured here in 1912.

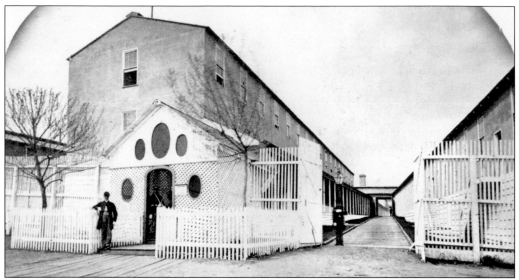

Open land adjacent to the Chestnut Hill Railroad made Chestnut Hill a good place for a large Civil War hospital. Mower General Hospital, also called Chestnut Hill Hospital, opened in 1863 on 27 acres between the railroad line and Stenton Avenue. The train station for the hospital was located where Wyndmoor Station now stands, before the rail line was elevated. John McArthur, architect of Philadelphia's city hall, designed the hospital complex in a series of radiating wards. This photograph shows the gatehouse and two of the 34 wards, which housed 20,000 patients before it closed its doors in 1865.

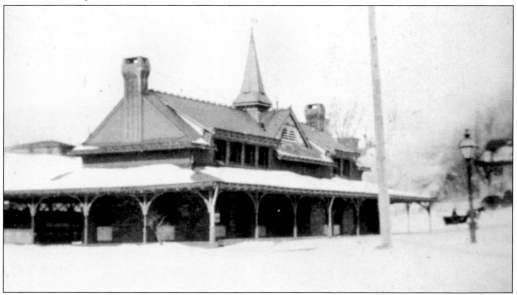

In 1884, Henry H. Houston opened the Pennsylvania Railroad line to the west side of Chestnut Hill to encourage the growth of his new development. This was the depot at the terminus, built in 1885 and shown here 10 years later. It was the former site of the Yeakel-Schultz barn, from which British soldiers stole stored liquor during the Revolutionary War. The rear of the Yeakel-Schultz house, now gone, is seen in the background along Germantown Avenue. Chestnut Hill station had separate waiting rooms for gentlemen and ladies. The spire and dormer were removed in the 20th century.

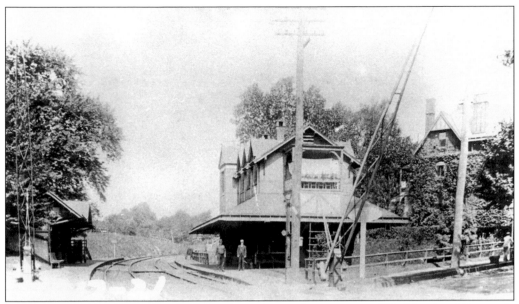

This is the former Highland Avenue station at the northeast corner of Highland and Seminole Avenues, when the railroad crossing was at grade (ground level). The house on the right is 309 West Highland Avenue and is still there today. One can see the cut made into the hill as the tracks turned the bend to the end of the line. In the 1890s, the ticket agent sold newspapers and candy as well as tickets. In 1916 or 1917, the Highland Avenue bridge was built to eliminate the grade crossing, and the station building was demolished. The lower picture looks south, away from Highland Avenue station, just as a steam engine is about to cross Highland Avenue. Tony, the one-legged crossing guard visible here, worked this corner 10 hours a day, lowering the gates across Germantown Avenue. The orchard indicates how rural Chestnut Hill still was c. 1895.

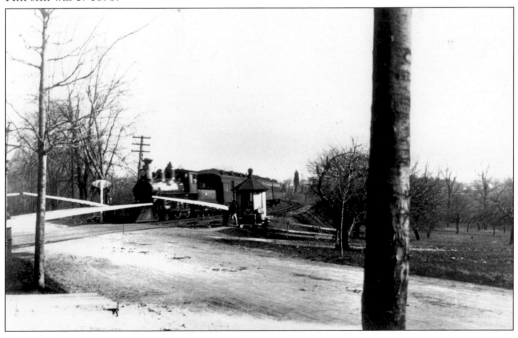

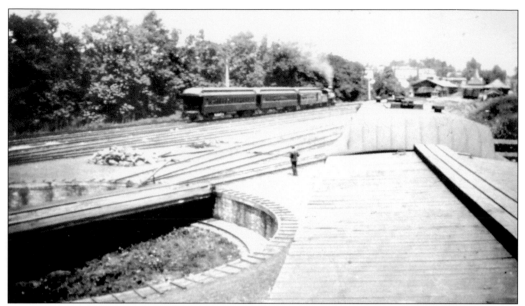

Turntables were needed to reverse the direction of the steam engines when they reached the end of the line at Chestnut Hill. The Pennsylvania line's turntable, shown here *c*. 1895 beside Evergreen Avenue, was built in 1884 and was replaced with a larger one in 1891. Men rotated the turntable manually by pushing against a cantilevered bar. They sometimes let neighborhood children "help" them push the turntable or sit in the engine as it was being turned. After the Pennsylvania Railroad was electrified in 1918, the turntable was phased out of service.

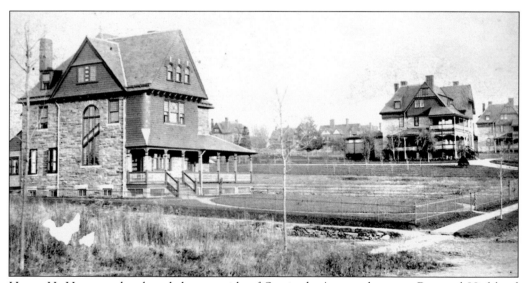

Henry H. Houston developed the east side of Seminole Avenue between Rex and Highland Avenues with these three houses designed by G.W. and W.D. Hewitt. The houses at 8635, 8605, and 8525 Seminole Avenue were newly built when this photograph was taken *c*. 1886. In the foreground, Seminole Avenue crosses Rex Avenue, which was then a small dirt lane. Lawns, a wood-plank sidewalk, and newly planted saplings along the avenue replaced the pastures that once filled this landscape. All three houses exist today, but the center one was refashioned into a Georgian Revival stone house.

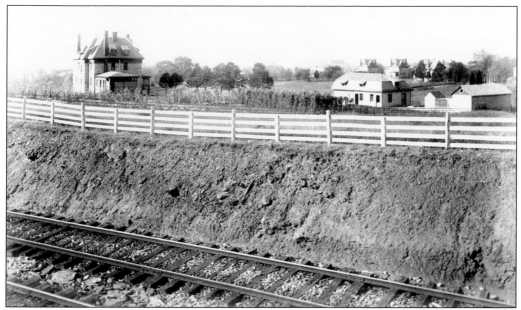

This was the rear view of 8605 Seminole Avenue (left) *c.* 1886 as seen from across the Pennsylvania Railroad tracks just north of Highland Station. In the right rear are three houses on Chestnut Hill Avenue, developed by Henry H. Houston from 1884 to 1885 as rental properties. The Hewitt brothers designed the two houses on the left and may have designed the one on the right. In the 1920s, the house on the left was moved to connect to the middle house, now 422 West Chestnut Hill Avenue.

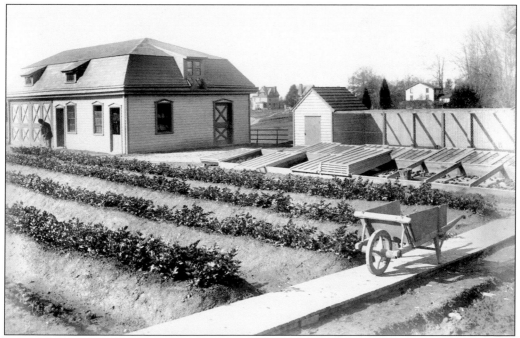

New suburbanites who sought to embrace country life with large gardens were by no means farmers, so they hired gardeners. This garden at 8605 Seminole Avenue had a garden shed, neat rows of vegetables, and extensive cold frames for nurturing new plants.

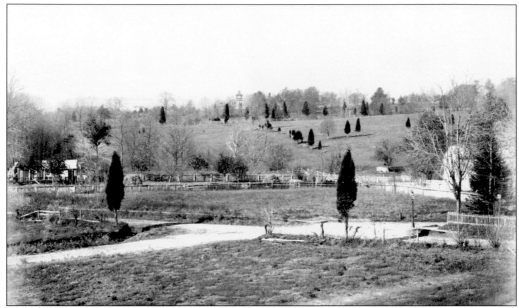

The contrast between rural Chestnut Hill and its sophisticated new estates may be seen in this c. 1886 photograph. This was the view across the Wissahickon Creek valley in what is now Fairmount Park near Thomas Mill Road and Chestnut Hill Avenue, looking north toward the hilltop at West Sunset Avenue. Villas like Belle Ayre (center) occupied the hilltops to command the views and to be seen. Belle Ayre is now gone, and the fields and farmhouses in the foreground have become public woodlands within Fairmount Park.

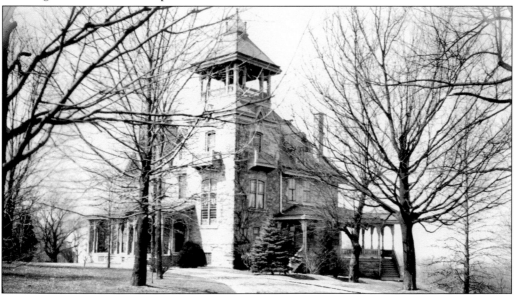

Banker George Bodine built Belle Ayre on Sunset Avenue in 1885. This villa was one of several homes in Chestnut Hill with an open tower, offering dramatic views of the Wissahickon and Whitemarsh Valleys. Its carriage house survives as a residence at 100 West Hampton Avenue. Belle Ayre was built before Crefeld Street was extended to meet Hampton Avenue. This photograph, taken between 1904 and 1910, looks west from Sunset Avenue along the estate's driveway.

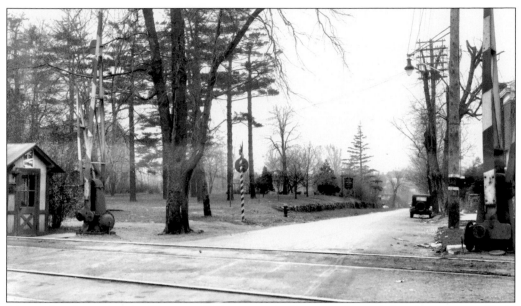

Most railroad crossings in Chestnut Hill were originally on grade until the increase in traffic in the early 20th century led to the construction of bridges. These photographs were taken looking west toward Germantown Avenue from the tracks at Mermaid Lane, with the 1929 view taken from grade, and the 1931 view taken from the newly constructed bridge over Mermaid Lane. In the earlier photograph (above), the crossing guard's shanty may be seen on the left, as well as Mermaid Hall, the Italianate stone house built in 1854–1855 for Theodore S. Williams. Mermaid Hall still exists, surrounded on three sides by adjoining buildings that now house the United Cerebral Palsy Association. Its rooftop is visible from the train today.

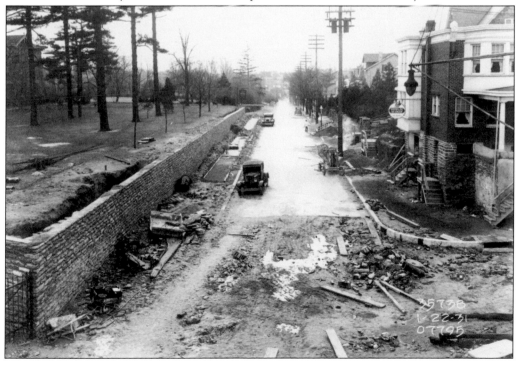

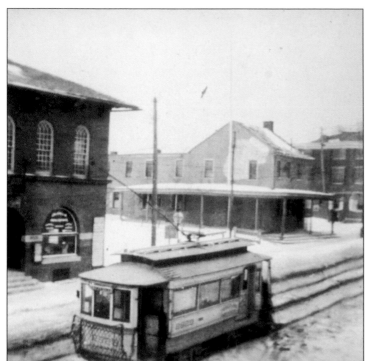

This trolley, or electric streetcar, is approaching Donat's Hotel at the southwest corner of Germantown and Highland Avenues. Levi Rex originally ran a temperance hotel there from 1800 to 1842, where alcohol was not served. Christian Donat was the next innkeeper, and he did serve alcohol. In Rex's day, farm wagons lined up in front of the inn as drovers spent the night and rested their horses en route from the country to Philadelphia. On the left is Joslin Hall (8434 Germantown Avenue), now the town hall.

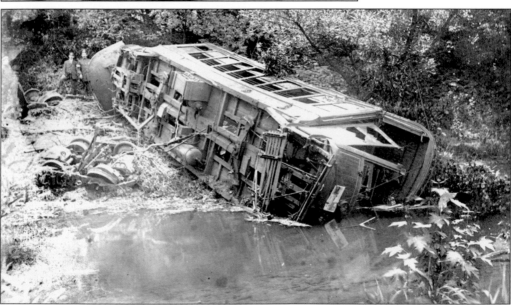

In 1913, the Route 23 trolley derailed when it hit a bundle of newspapers on the tracks on the Germantown Avenue bridge. Trolley man Felix Henry surveys the damage. Trolleys came to the top of the hill in 1894 and to Northwestern Avenue and Erdenheim in 1898, but not without controversy. Chestnut Hillers held an "Anti-Trolley Meeting and Banquet" at the Wissahickon Inn for the mayor and councilmen in 1894. When John Welsh, president of the Union Traction Company, started laying trolley tracks down Bethlehem Pike, a group of residents removed them during the night and deposited them in Welsh's front yard in Wyndmoor. Welsh rerouted the trolley down Hillcrest Avenue to the White City amusement park in Erdenheim.

Three

THE WORKING TOWN

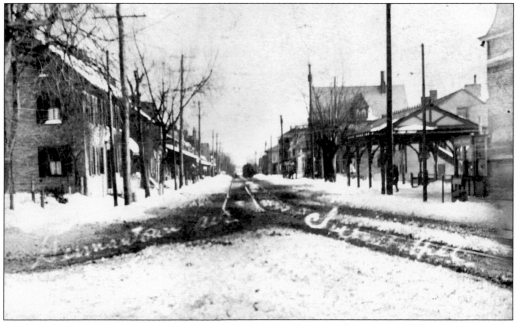

Mud and snow mix on an unpaved Germantown Avenue, known as Main Street at the beginning of the 20th century. The view looks south from the fork of Germantown Avenue and Bethlehem Pike. On the right is the wooden pavilion above the Pennsylvania Railroad terminus, erected in 1892 for a newsstand run by the Union News Company. Behind the pavilion is the Yeakel-Schultz house, replaced by a gas station in 1965 and now stores. A trolley passes a wagon on the quiet street.

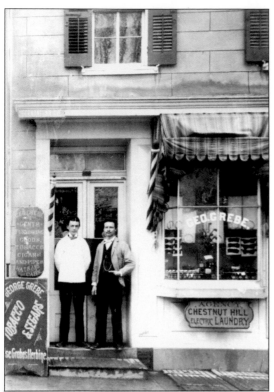

Barber George Grebe opened this "gents furnishing goods" store in 1892 at 8527 Germantown Avenue (also visible in the photograph to the right) and moved across the street in 1897. Detachable collars, ties, hats, and "segars" were available for purchase. The storefront today has a stone façade and enlarged windows. Shopkeepers tended to live above their storefronts in Chestnut Hill. Just south of this store, Samuel Saur published the first known Chestnut Hill newspaper from 1790 to 1794, called *Die Chesnuthiller Wochenschrift,* meaning "The Chestnut Hill Weekly Newspaper."

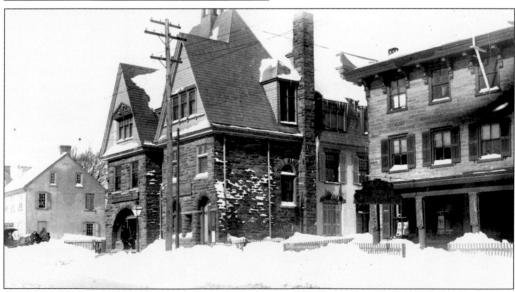

At the property on the right in 1812, Charles Redheffer charged $5 for men ("female visitors gratis") to see his perpetual motion machine, which caused such a sensation that the city council appointed a committee to see if the machine really worked. Redheffer left for New York, and his invention was revealed as a hoax when it was discovered that a hidden man turned a crank. The Masonic building in the center (8427 Germantown Avenue) was built in 1889 for the Knights of Pythias fraternal order. Now covered over, the stone arches are still visible in this photograph.

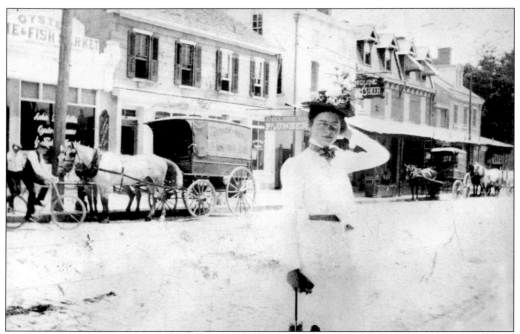

A woman shows off her fetching spring bonnet and parasol on the 8500 block of Germantown Avenue *c.* 1910 (above). In the background, a cyclist passes the delivery wagon for Gillies Oyster, Game & Fish Market as it stands ready to make its rounds. Gillies was in business from 1887 to 1961. In the lower photograph, John L. Gillies's fleet of trucks waits in front of their other store down the block at 8515 Germantown Avenue in the mid-1920s. One only had to "phone Chestnut Hill 961," as indicated on the side of the windshield-less truck, to have one's items hauled. By this time, electric streetcars had been running on Chestnut Hill's rails (foreground) for some 25 years, yet Chestnut Hill still had open spaces along Germantown Avenue.

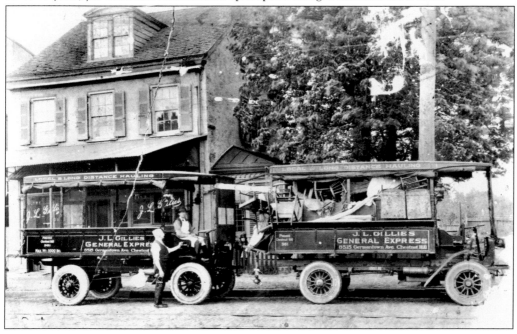

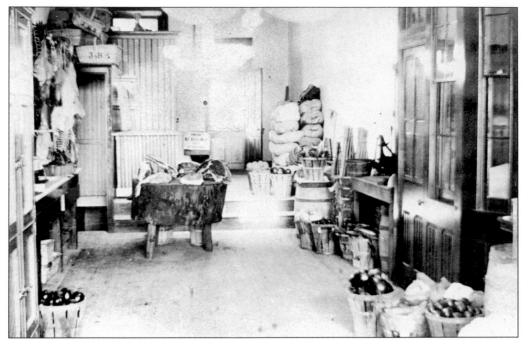

Buckingham's store, located at the northeast corner of Evergreen and Germantown Avenues and shown here in the 1890s, sold freshly butchered meats and bushel baskets of vegetables. The basket up high on the left bears the owner's initials, J.B. As refrigeration was rudimentary and transportation for many was by foot, there were several provisioners of food along Germantown Avenue. This building stands on the former site of the marble yard of Harry Miller.

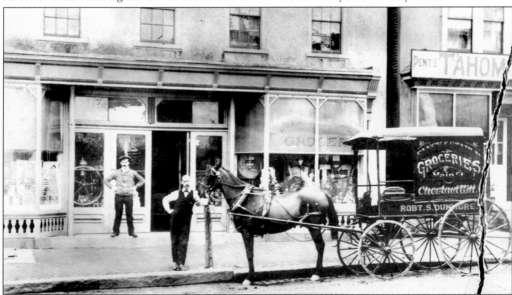

Robert Dunmore kept this grocery store at 8416 Germantown Avenue, seen here in 1908. James Neiler is beside the door. Deliveryman William Woodruff, leaning against a hitching post, began working at Dunmore's around age 14, eventually driving this wagon and later a delivery truck. "Willie" grew up on his uncle's sheep farm across Germantown Avenue from where the Jenks School is today. To the right is McNamee's Cigar Store, now Caruso's Market.

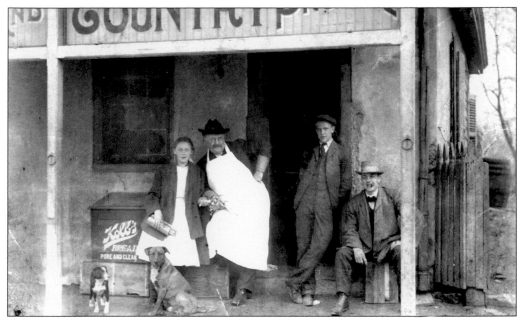

In this *c.* 1905 photograph, Ethel and Russell Aiman flank their father, John Aiman, who wears butcher's cuffs on his arms. The family lived above this butcher and grocery shop at the southeast corner of Springfield and Germantown Avenues. Kolb's Bakery delivered bread at 5 a.m. to the unlocked box beside Ethel. Seated is butcher Wesley Titus Shantz, a friend of Aiman's. Shantz was also a friend of John Sergeant Price Jr., a noted horseman who taught him to drive four-in-hand carriages (see pages 58 and 109). Children were entertained watching Aiman cut up meat on the stump of a tree outside the store.

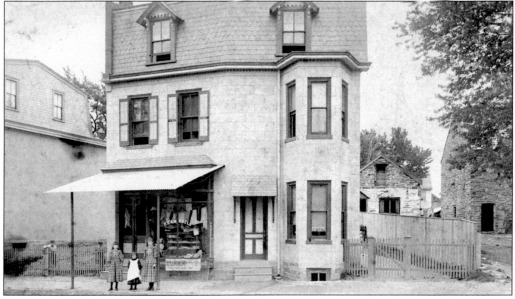

This stuccoed building with its unusual angled façade was built in 1891 for Patrick Campbell's Laundry and is now Bredenbeck's Bakery and Ice Cream Store. Tin awnings to protect customers from sun and rain were once common features on Germantown Avenue stores. The small stone building to the rear is now incorporated into the larger Stagecrafters building.

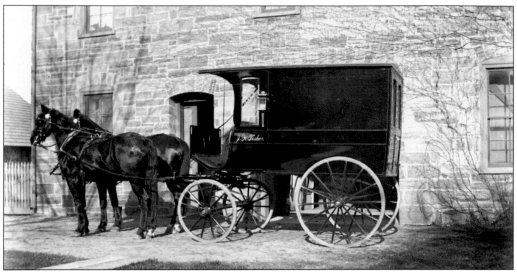

The first building erected at 8413 Germantown Avenue in 1887, where Jacob F. Ruth Funeral Directors Inc. is today, was the workshop in the rear, pictured above behind the J.H. Fisher hearse carriage in the 1890s. Titus Shermer built coffins as part of his furniture business at Germantown Avenue and Hartwell Lane in the first half of the 19th century. Shermer sold the business to William Fisher in the 1850s. The business gradually evolved from coffin making to undertaking. William's son Jacob is seen below shoveling snow *c.* 1905 in front of the home with his employee, James Gold, who worked for the Fishers for about 50 years. Across the street is Trinity Presbyterian Church (see page 85), peeking out from behind a house that was demolished in 1926 for a church driveway. The church was later demolished.

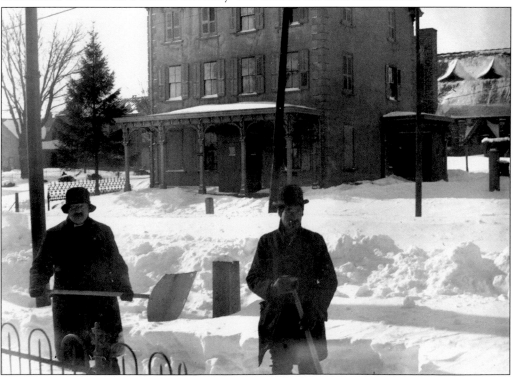

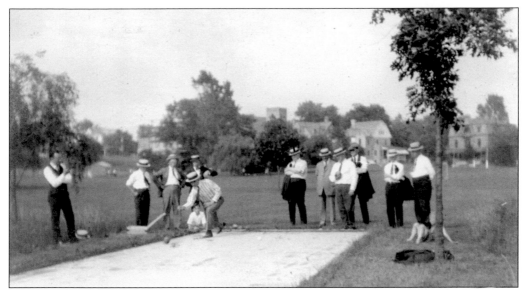

Members of the Germantown and Chestnut Hill Improvement Association play bocce at their outing in 1906. The association tackled problems and lobbied city hall for improvements to the 22nd Ward, which included Chestnut Hill, Mount Airy, and Germantown. Among the more than 300 members was Walter A. Dwyer, a coal merchant, as well as George Woodward. The association's accomplishments included successfully lobbying for the construction of elevated train crossings and building the John Story Jenks Public Elementary School. (Courtesy Germantown Historical Society.)

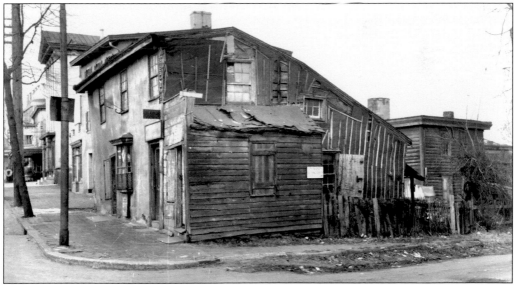

Not all storeowners were prosperous. "Mommy" Gable's candy shop was on the northeast corner of Germantown Avenue and Hartwell Lane c. 1900. Mommy sold the best marbles and other items children coveted. The building was condemned by the city and demolished in 1931. Up Germantown Avenue from the leaning wall of the second building is Hiram Lodge Masonic Hall (at 8217 Germantown Avenue), constructed in 1859 and now the Veterans of Foreign Wars building. The corner tower of the Chestnut Hill Hotel may be seen up the hill. Buckley Park now occupies the site of Gable's and the next building.

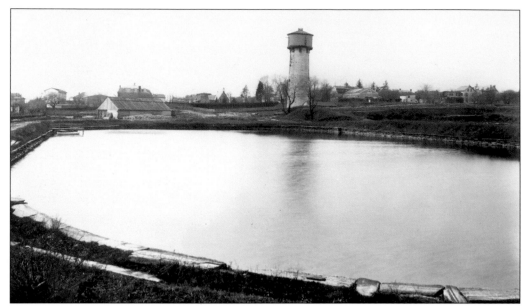

The Chestnut Hill Water Company built this water tower in 1859. The City of Philadelphia's water system did not extend to Chestnut Hill. The photographer of this 1896 view was standing about where the water tower playground is today, looking west toward Germantown Avenue. The stone-lined basin, which was about 20 feet deep, was where the playing field is today. In the distance to the left one can see the rear of the Chestnut Hill Hotel and Christ Lutheran Church. Water from the reservoir was pumped up into the tower, creating water pressure when it was released. Untreated water was piped to customers, requiring it to be boiled before use. In 1904, the Philadelphia Water Department began pumping treated water to Chestnut Hill from the Schuylkill River, making this pumping station obsolete.

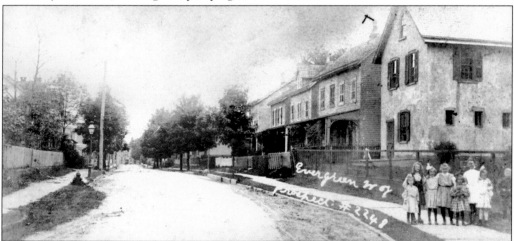

Smaller houses, many of them twins, were clustered along the cross streets of Germantown Avenue. Many were the homes of tradespeople, shopkeepers, and people who worked in the large houses. Girls sporting large bows in their hair, as was the style c. 1910, pose for this photograph on the sidewalk of East Evergreen Avenue, looking west toward Germantown Avenue just west of Prospect Street. One girl clutches her doll and another a stuffed toy. The first house on the right no longer exists. Streeper's drugstore is visible in the distance on the southwest corner of Germantown and Evergreen Avenues.

With its hairpin fence, so common in Chestnut Hill, 8442 Ardleigh Street looks much the same today as it did in 1908, when this Dutch Colonial Revival house was built. The rear of the Masonic building is visible on the left. The building on the right, fronting on an unpaved Highland Avenue, is now gone.

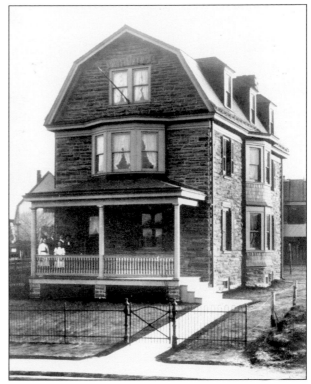

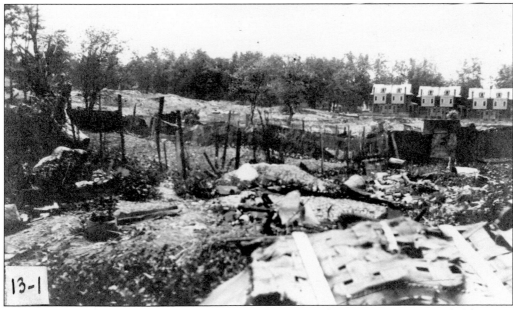

The City of Philadelphia converted an 85-foot-deep quarry between Winston Road, Abington Avenue, and East Willow Grove Avenue into a dump *c.* 1940. Refuse attracted rats and caused a terrible problem for the residents of the 8100 block of Ardleigh Street and others who lived nearby. The city eventually cleared the dump and filled the quarry. Apartments, houses, and the Water Tower Recreation Center tennis courts now take its place. This photograph looks south across the dump toward the rear of the houses at 201 to 211 East Willow Grove Avenue.

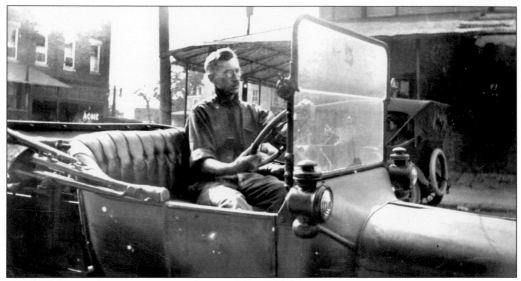

Russell Goudy, pictured here between 1920 and 1923, made deliveries in this Model T Ford for his brother-in-law, William Kilian. The automobile is in front of the tin awning of what is now Robertson Florists. William A. Kilian Hardware Company was begun in 1913 at 8605 Germantown Avenue. After William died in 1938, his wife, Minnie, ran the business with another brother, John Nelson Goudy. His son Russell Goudy and family run the store today.

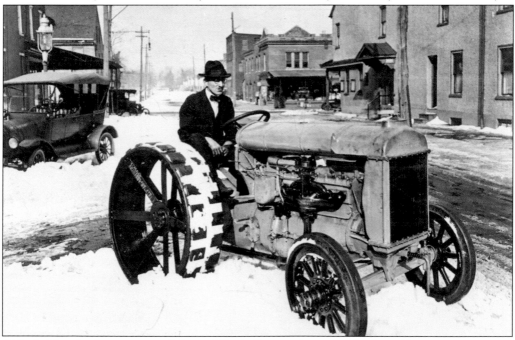

Alfred Allan had just emerged from Allan's Garage driving a Fordson Company tractor on the first block of West Highland Avenue when this photograph was taken in 1922. To the right is the former Donat's Hotel, the site of Kilian's hardware store today, at the southwest corner of Germantown and Highland Avenues. After Prohibition ruined the saloon business at this corner for Gaiser, the Kilians purchased the property and had Melvin Grebe build a new building on the site in 1925.

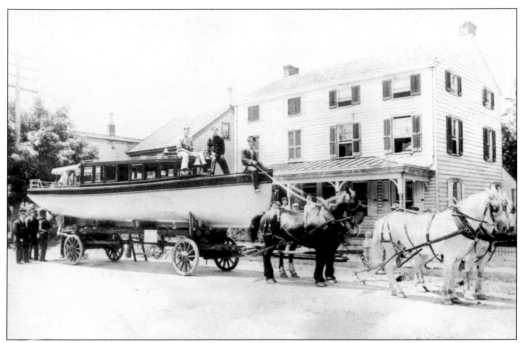

Ephraim Jones, holding the reins, was a Chestnut Hill fireman who built this boat, the *Highland*, in the second story of the Chestnut Hill firehouse *c.* 1910. Part of the wall had to be removed to get the boat out. The *Highland* was launched on the Delaware River and is still seaworthy today. The rooftop of the Temperance Hall building can be seen to the left at the northeast corner of Highland Avenue and Shawnee Street. The Sons of Temperance, established in 1844, pledged to not drink liquor and to influence stores and hotels not to sell or serve spirits.

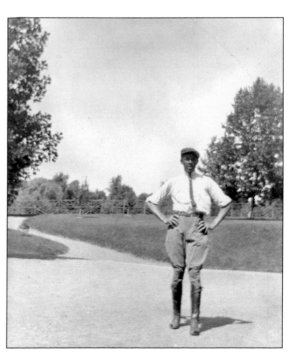

Many jobs in Chestnut Hill were off Germantown Avenue at estates surrounding the village, which needed staffs to make them function. George Cloverdale was the chauffeur for the Clark family *c.* 1915 (see page 68). In the early days of the automobile, a chauffeur's job involved much more than driving. Early cars had to be maintained constantly because of the wear and tear of driving on dirt roads. The chauffeur was also the automobile mechanic, since he had to install new parts ordered by mail from the factory.

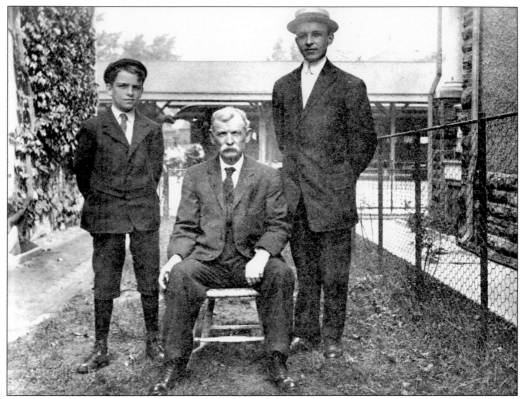

Edward Dwyer came from Ireland in the late 1830s or 1840s and lived in North Philadelphia until the mid-1850s. He bought Jones's Coal Yard in 1875 at the corner of Bethlehem Pike and New Street, now Newton Street. He built a house across the tracks from Dwyer's Coal Yard at 124 East Chestnut Hill Avenue in 1885. Pictured above are Edward's son, Walter A. Dwyer, and his sons Walter T. (left) and Edward. Their White Motorcar Company truck (below), which delivered building materials as well as coal, dates from c. 1915. To start the truck, you turned a crank at the front and had to quickly release it when the engine started or risk a broken wrist. Note the cast-iron wheels, gas light fixture, tool chest on the running board, and windowless cab.

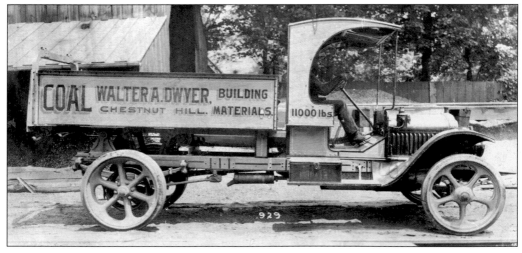

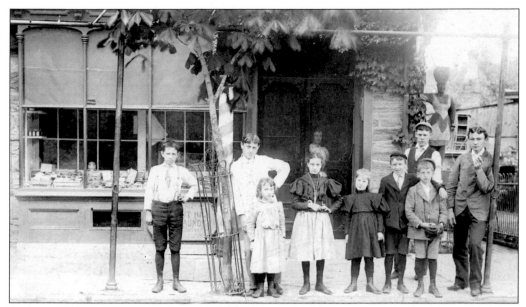

Built c. 1870 as a barn structure, probably for 101 Bethlehem Pike, this building at 45 East Chestnut Hill Avenue soon became a commercial property. Conrad Grebe's Barbershop, complete with striped barber pole, displays the sign "Fancy Chestnut Hill Laundry" c. 1892. Edward Dwyer (see page 48) has his arm around the boy with the baseball and glove. Elsie Grebe overlooks the scene from the doorway, along with the wooden Indian woman to the right of the building. Alice Lee later ran a bakery and ice-cream store here, where William Dwyer, Edward's nephew, worked and sampled the goods in the 1930s.

Andorra Nurseries, founded by Henry H. Houston in 1886, was purchased by its business manager, William Warner Harper, after Houston's death in 1895. Under Harper's leadership, Andorra became the largest commercial nursery in the northeastern United States, covering more than 1,000 acres in Philadelphia and adjoining Montgomery County. Harper's astute marketing, which included lavish brochures like this one, was a major reason for Andorra's success. The nurseries closed in 1961. Today, part of the original Houston property is the Andorra Natural Area, while the rest of the nursery was developed for homes. (Courtesy Germantown Historical Society.)

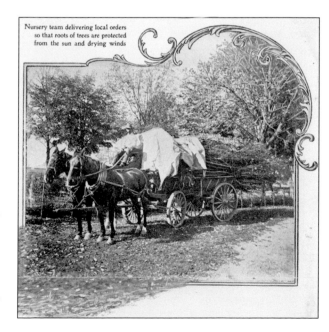

Nursery team delivering local orders so that roots of trees are protected from the sun and drying winds

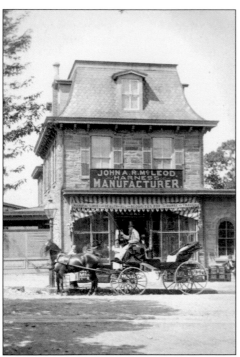

Germantown harness maker John McLeod produced this trade card c. 1879. A fine carriage and neat row of trunks are displayed in front of his branch store at 101 Bethlehem Pike, built c. 1870. McNaughton's store, which made candy and ice cream, later occupied this building. Around 1900, Springside School girls would come around the corner to buy ice-cream sodas here. A girl got a soda glass next door at Whittem's Pharmacy, filled it with ice cream at McNaughton's, and then returned to Whittem's for the soda.

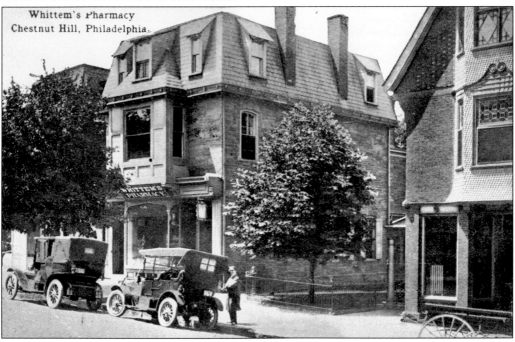

These two buildings on the 100 block of Bethlehem Pike were built in 1888, and both housed businesses that lasted for over a century. William A. Whittem located his pharmacy here because he believed a business district would flourish near the railroad terminus. His son Bill, as a boy, rendered curbside delivery service to ladies in their carriages who did not want to make the trip into the store. To the right is Charles E. Hopkin stoves and heaters, whose business thrives 114 years later as a roofing company.

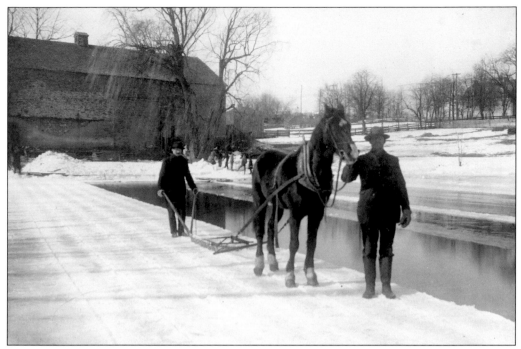

Casey's Ice Pond was located where Lincoln Drive now crosses Springfield Avenue. The photograph above, looking northwest toward Willow Grove Avenue c. 1910, shows the icehouse, which was built in 1843. James Casey, owner of the Chestnut Hill Ice Company, leads a horse with a cutting device on the ice. Ice blocks were stacked in the icehouse and packed in sawdust until they were loaded onto railroad cars on a siding at St. Martin's Station. Casey's two ponds were popular with skaters, who were charged 5¢ to skate (below). The back of his house, 230 West Willow Grove Avenue, can be seen in the distance, with wash drying in the yard. To the right is Henry D. Welsh's towered home (see page 57), and to the left the steeple of St. Martin-in-the-Fields Church.

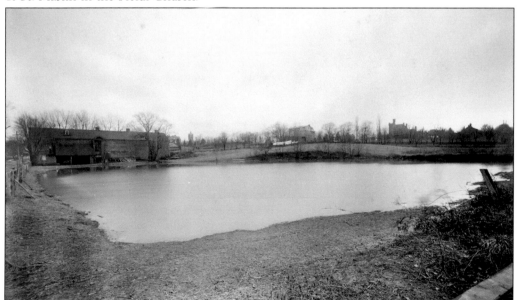

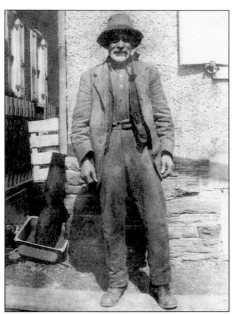

Luigi Serianni, born in Calabria, Italy, in 1848, came to Philadelphia in 1886 and worked as a stonemason at the Chestnut Hill Quarry on East Mermaid Lane. Serianni protested unsuccessfully in 1915 when the City of Philadelphia demolished his home at 124 West Hartwell Lane to make way for Pastorius Park. George Woodward offered the city nine acres of land he owned to create the park, provided the city would condemn two adjoining acres and remove the houses. Serianni's projects included work at Our Mother of Consolation Church and Whitemarsh Hall.

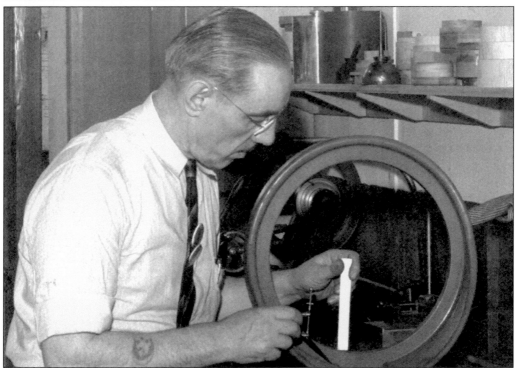

Guiseppe Spallone, born in Italy in 1890, changed his name to Joseph after coming to America and moving to Chestnut Hill. He was a master carpenter who "could fashion almost anything out of almost anything" and who first worked at the Venetian Club. Around 1933, when he heard that Philo T. Farnsworth, the inventor of television, was setting up a research laboratory, Spallone applied for a job and was hired on the spot. He is pictured in Farnsworth's lab, which was located at 127 East Mermaid Lane and later in Wyndmoor. Joseph's daughter Lucy married Luigi Serianni's grandson.

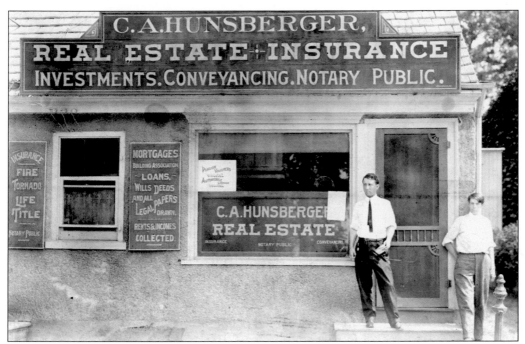

Charles Hunsberger (born 1872) was a real estate agent and developer who built three sets of twin houses on the north side of the 200 and 300 block of East Gravers Lane. Here he stands in front of his office at 8609 Germantown Avenue, built in 1914. Charles served in the Spanish-American War and was wounded in the head as he went up San Juan Hill in Cuba with Theodore Roosevelt. Until he married, Charles rented a room at the Maple Lawn Inn, called the Dust Pan, at the fork of Germantown Avenue and Bethlehem Pike.

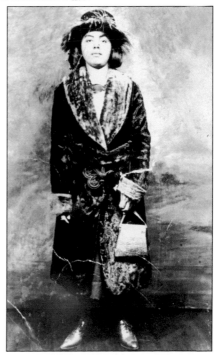

Bessie Miles, born in 1904 and pictured here as a teenager, grew up on her father's prosperous Virginia farm and came to Chestnut Hill in 1935 to be near her brother and his wife. She worked in the Chestnut Hill Community Centre bakery, supporting her six children on her own. For $16 a month, she rented the house at 150 East Hartwell Lane, with a pot-bellied stove and one cold water tap. Bessie, a member of the NAACP, counseled her children to "be careful because you're colored, don't complain, and help yourself." Her son Rudy's best friend was Buddy Morasco, an Italian-American boy who did not care that his friend was from one of the few black families in the neighborhood. Rudy recalled that it meant a lot to him that Buddy treated his mother with respect when he came to her door.

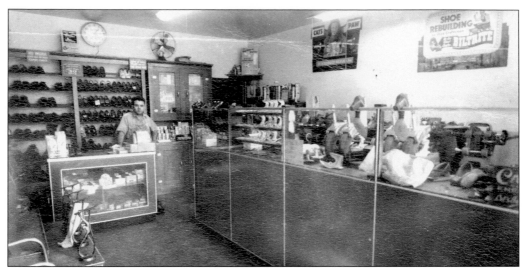

Carmen Notarianni Sr. began this shoe-repair shop in 1939 at 8113 Germantown Avenue. It is pictured here in the early 1950s. His father, Pietro, left southern Italy in 1934 because of the uncertain political situation. Carmen was 17 then and had learned the shoe-repair trade in Italy. He continued with his trade during World War II in the U.S. Army while a hired man ran the shop for him. His son Carmen Jr. joined him, and the shop moved next door to 8111 Germantown Avenue in 1997.

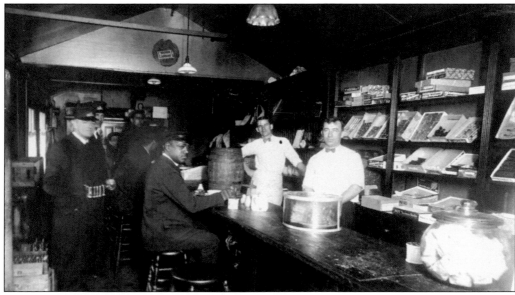

Pictured c. 1923 is McNally's Light Lunch, across from 8634 Germantown Avenue, where McNally's Tavern is today. Hugh McNally was a Philadelphia Rapid Transit (PRT) trolley driver. His wife, Rose O'Brien, observed that PRT workers needed a lunchroom in Chestnut Hill. They got permission to open a restaurant on PRT property and moved to Chestnut Hill from Fishtown in 1921. Prohibition was in effect, so only "Barge's Better Beverages" and the like were served. This was one of the few restaurants in Chestnut Hill that served African Americans. The man seated in the foreground was probably a chauffeur. In 1927, the McNallys bought the present building, which became a tavern in 1933 after Prohibition was lifted. Pictured are Rose and Hugh's sons, John, left, and Hugh McNally II.

Four

GREAT HOUSES
AND ESTATES

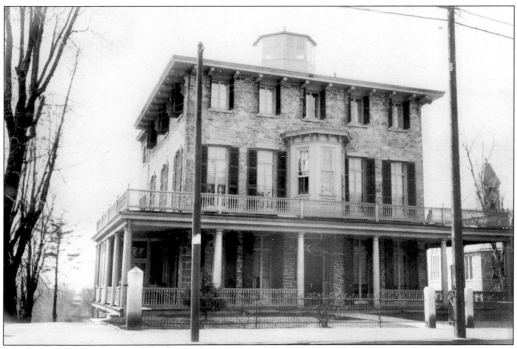

Once the railroad reached Chestnut Hill in 1854, many affluent Philadelphians established summer or year-round estates there. One early resident was Caleb Cope, president of the Philadelphia Savings Fund Society from 1864 until 1888. Cope owned this Italianate stone house at the southwest corner of Germantown and Rex Avenues (8630–8640 Germantown Avenue). Lavish gardens, open to the public, stretched behind his house to Crefeld Street, including a natural spring that ran through "Cope's Grotto." As Germantown Avenue grew more commercial, large estates moved farther away from it. The Cope House was torn down in the early 20th century and replaced by stores; the gardens behind it were converted to housing lots.

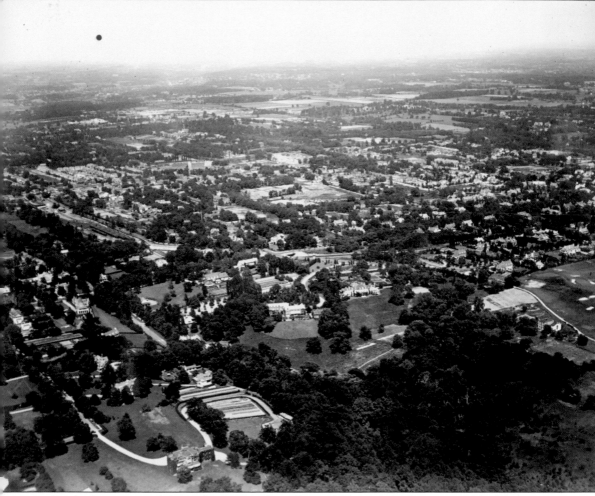

By the beginning of the 20th century, the village of Chestnut Hill was ringed by large estates, many of which were self-contained, working farms. This aerial view of Chestnut Hill in the 1920s shows the estates lining Seminole Avenue and St. Martin's Lane near the Chestnut Hill West railroad line. Shown from left to right are Norwood Hall, home of the Jacob Disston family; Kate's Hall, home of the Joseph Sill Clark family; and Boxly, home of Frederick W. Taylor, founder of industrial management. At the far right are Hartwell Lane and the golf course of the Philadelphia Cricket Club.

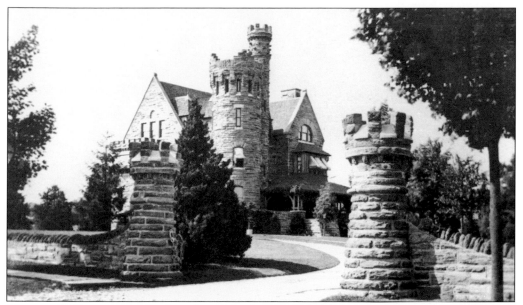

Chestnut Hill's west side developed quickly after the Philadelphia, Germantown, and Chestnut Hill railroad line of the Pennsylvania Railroad opened in 1884. Henry D. Welsh, partner to Henry H. Houston and president of the Chestnut Hill line, built his house, Seminole, at the northeast corner of Willow Grove and Seminole Avenues in 1887–1888 (see page 51). G.W. and W.D. Hewitt designed the house, which was demolished in the 1920s.

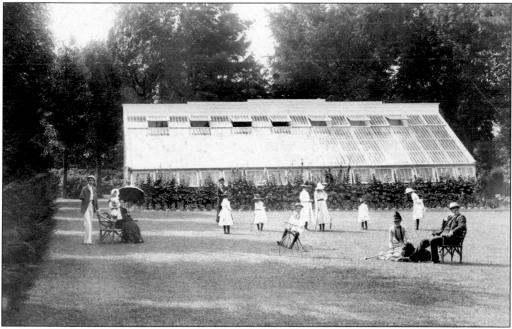

The Albert Kelseys lived at Rauhala at 8765 Stenton Avenue. In this 1890 photograph, Mr. and Mrs. Albert Kelsey sit in rustic armchairs while their children and grandchildren play croquet in front of the estate greenhouse. The young man on the left has his arm in a sling. A note on the photograph explains that "Albert at St. Luke's fell from a cherry tree broke his collar bone and arm." Today, Keystone Hospice occupies the site.

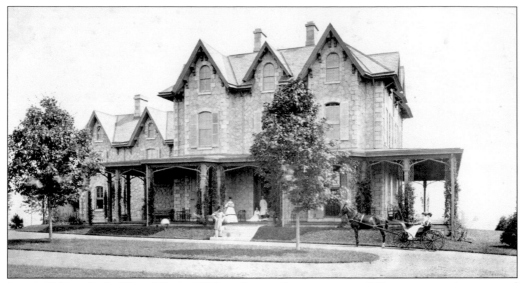

Joseph F. Page built Wyncliffe in 1875 at the northwest corner of Germantown Avenue and Bell's Mill Road. It stood atop a hill named Sugarloaf by early settlers who thought it resembled a loaf of sugar. In 1953, real estate developer Albert M. Greenfield purchased the adjacent property, also named Sugarloaf, and had it redesigned by Edward Durrell Stone. In 1958, Greenfield purchased Wyncliffe from Sophie DuPont (Mrs. Bruce) Ford. After Greenfield's death, his family foundation donated the entire 30-acre Sugarloaf-Wyncliffe property to Temple University, which operates it today as the Albert M. Greenfield Conference Center.

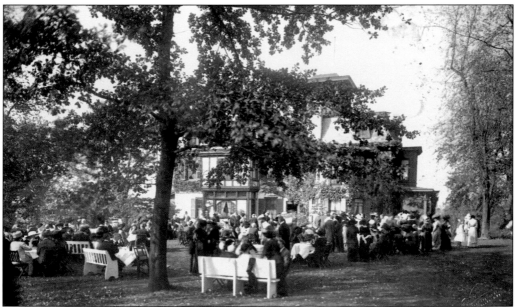

Edgecombe, at 139 Bethlehem Pike, was converted from a farmhouse to a country house for the marriage of Sallie Baker and John Sergeant Price in 1856. Their youngest son, John Sergeant Price Jr., lived there until his death in 1948. Price, a noted horseman, held cockfights in the billiard room of Edgecombe, built a tennis court (which he flooded for skating in the winter), and staged outdoor dinners with champagne and terrapin in the snow. This photograph, taken c. 1915, shows an afternoon garden party at Edgecombe.

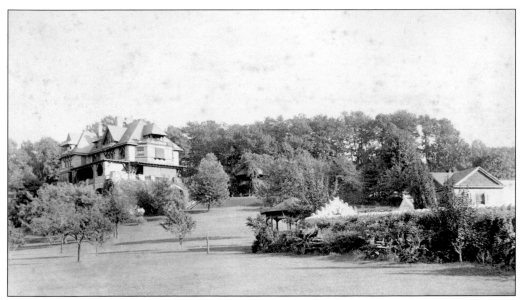

Stonecliffe, at Norwood and East Sunset Avenues, was designed in 1880 by Theophilus P. Chandler for Mrs. Charles (Mary) Taylor, widow of the developer of Norwood Avenue. A porch wrapped around three sides of the house, offering views of the Whitemarsh Valley and the distant Reading hills. After Mrs. Taylor died in 1890, the estate was purchased by Drexel, Morgan investment banker George C. Thomas and renamed Greystock after his former home in Wyndmoor. The photograph above shows Greystock, with its walled garden and summer house in the right foreground c. 1890. The photograph below shows George Thomas's daughter Sophie driving "Don," with groom Ben, c. 1894. Sophie later married Schuyler Volkmar and lived at Greystock until her death in the early 1960s. The house exists today in a highly altered state, and the property has been subdivided.

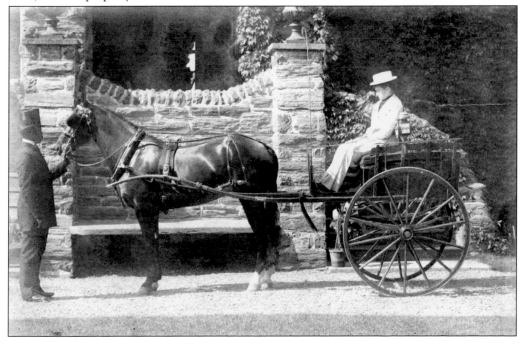

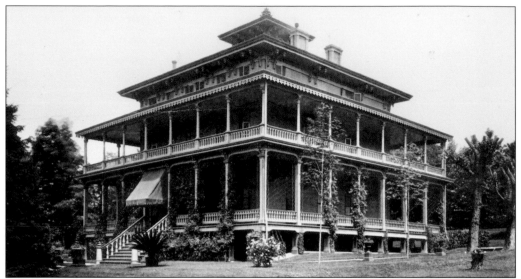

In 1869, Thomas Potter bought the Evergreens on Stenton Avenue between Summit Street and Evergreen Avenue (see page 26). Potter, a self-made man, left school at age 11 to become a wealthy manufacturer, banker, and philanthropist. Two of his sons later lived nearby: Charles built Anglecot on the rear of his father's property, and William lived at Stenton Avenue and Gravers Lane. The Evergreens was demolished between 1900 and 1911.

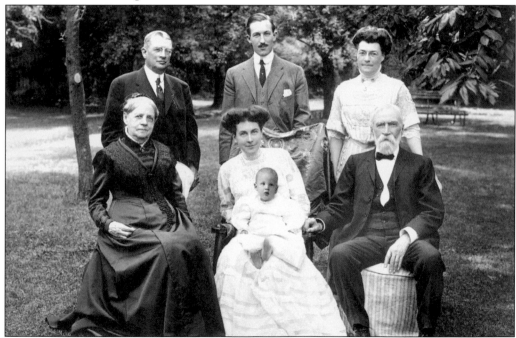

This 1909 portrait shows, from left to right, the following: (standing) Thomas Potter Jr., eldest son of the Evergreens owner; his son Wilson Potter; and his wife, Lily; (seated) Wilson's mother-in-law Martha Wilson; his wife Charlotte, holding their son Rust; and his father-in-law Seth Wilson. Unfortunately, this happy group would not last—Wilson's son Rust was struck and killed by a car in 1918. Wilson and Charlotte divorced in 1920. Wilson's second wife divorced and sued him, leaving him to die alone in his Alden Park apartment in 1946.

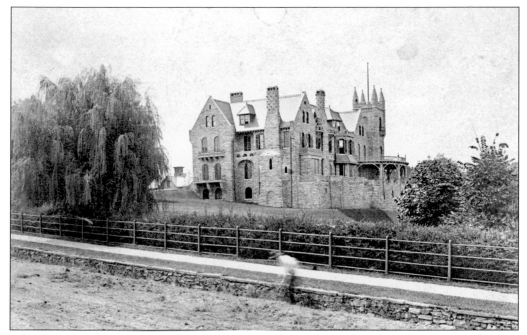

After his first home burned, Edwin N. Benson hired Theophilus P. Chandler to design a fireproof castle of stone, concrete, and steel. Lynnewood Hall, built in 1884 at 185 Bethlehem Pike, was one of the largest and most expensive mansions in Chestnut Hill. After the house was demolished in 1940, the site was used for the Chestnut Hill Hospital Main Street Fair. Only its large stone gateposts on Bethlehem Pike remain.

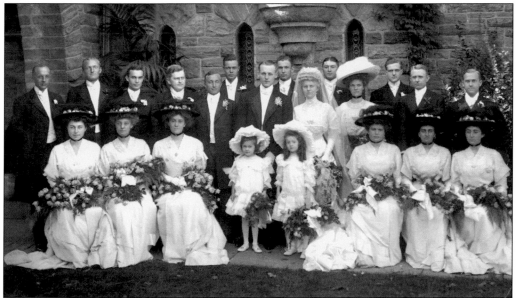

Mildred Benson, youngest daughter of Edwin N. Benson Sr., married John H. Packard III on October 8, 1907. The wedding party, shown here in front of the porte-cochere at Lynnewood Hall, included members of the Beale, Cadwallader, Curtis, Frazer, Ingersoll, Meade, Meigs, Newbold, Newhall, and Rodman families. The bride and groom were the great-grandparents of Bowman Properties founder Richard Snowden.

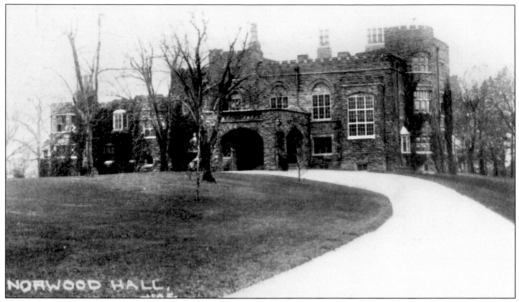

Norwood Hall, at West Chestnut Hill Avenue and Towanda Street, was designed by George T. Pearson for Chancellor C. English. In 1909, the 25-room mansion on an 18-acre estate was purchased for $175,000 by Jacob Disston, one of the heirs to the Henry Disston & Sons saw-manufacturing fortune. After that, the Gothic structure was also known as Disston's Castle. It was demolished in the 1930s and replaced by more contemporary houses.

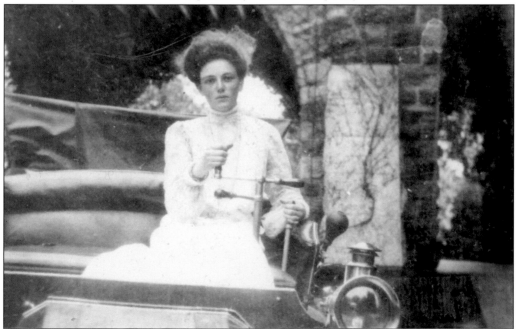

Lucy Disston, shown in the porte-cochere of Norwood Hall *c.* 1910, was a star field hockey player for the Springside School and the Philadelphia Cricket Club. She and her sisters Dorothy, Effie, and Marie won many championships, including the annual Cricket Club Christmas Day match against men dressed in skirts. She has her hand on the crank of an Autocar, an early automobile manufactured in nearby Ardmore.

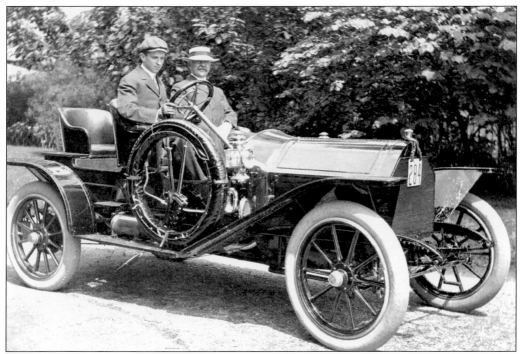

Dr. Radcliffe Cheston, a wealthy physician, was a cofounder and the first president of Chestnut Hill Hospital. He was also a consulting physician for the Home for Consumptives on Stenton Avenue (see pages 96–97). The photograph above, taken by his daughter Lilly, shows Cheston and his son Radcliffe Jr. in a 1910 Cadillac. Only prosperous families like the Chestons, Disstons, Kelseys, and Glendinnings could afford cars before the heyday of the Model T. Of 50 cars made by Ford in 1901, one was sold to a Chestnut Hill resident for $1,400—nearly three times the annual salary of the average worker. The Radcliffe Cheston residence (shown below), designed by Cope & Stewardson and built in 1890, still stands at 102 West Chestnut Hill Avenue.

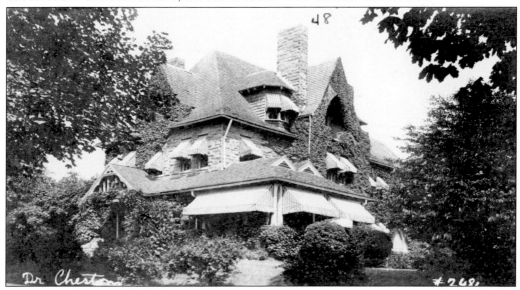

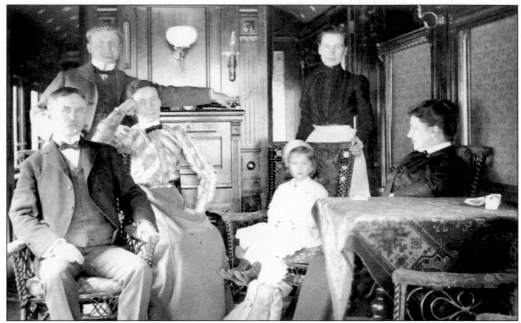

Some Chestnut Hillers preferred the train. Henry Houston Kingston, president of the Investment Company of Philadelphia, had a private railroad car, No. 354. Shown in the car on a March 1900 trip are, from left to right, Kingston, son William, cousin Julia Spackman, daughter Marion with doll, nurse Sarah, and wife Fannie. The Kingstons lived at Sherwood (at 8015 St. Martin's Lane), a Georgian Revival house designed by George T. Pearson.

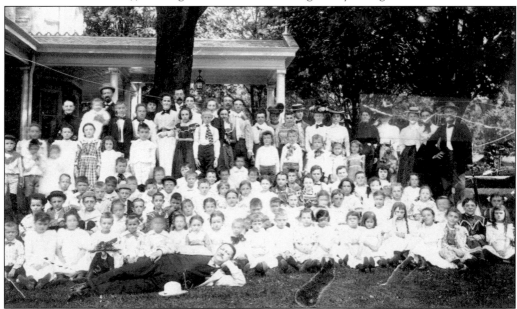

After Charles Knox Smith made a fortune in oil and mining, he purchased a nine-acre estate named Woodmere at 9201 Germantown Avenue (see page 24). He added a two-story rotunda gallery to the Italianate villa to house his collection of 600 paintings, European porcelain, rugs, and Oriental artwork. The photograph above, taken c. 1910, shows Smith lying in the foreground at a picnic at Woodmere, possibly for orphans from the nearby Bethesda Home.

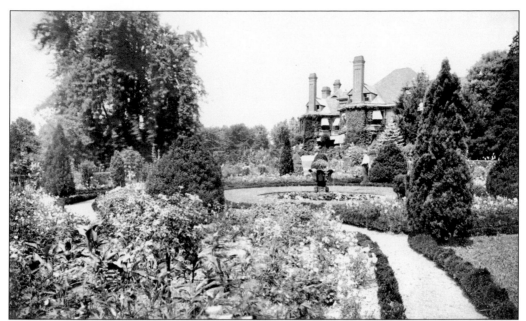

Around 1900, Randal Morgan, partner in the law firm of Morgan & Lewis and counsel for the United Gas Improvement Company, purchased an 85-acre property in East Chestnut Hill that he called Wyndmoor. The estate, bordered by East Willow Grove Avenue, Stenton Avenue, Mermaid Lane, and the Reading Railroad, encompassed the Civil War site of the Mower Hospital (see page 30). Morgan built a large house facing Willow Grove Avenue; the rest of the property was covered by lavish gardens and a working farm. The estate shared its name with a nearby town on the Montgomery County side of Stenton Avenue, formerly named Spring Village. After much controversy, the Morgan estate was developed in the 1950s and 1960s. Today, Chestnut Hill Village, Market Square, and the Hilltower Apartments cover the site.

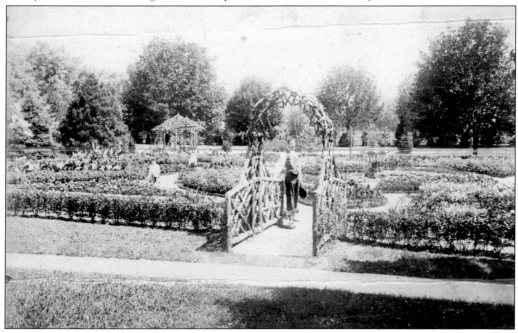

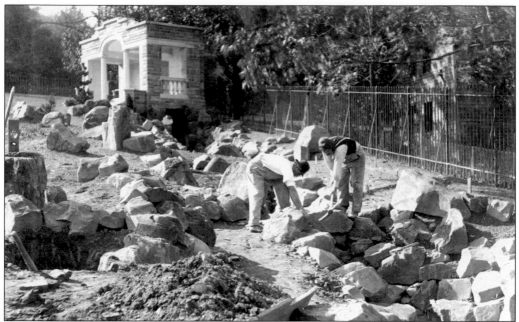

John and Lydia Morris, brother and sister heirs to an ironworks fortune, purchased a Chestnut Hill farm, which they named Compton, in 1887. Theophilus P. Chandler designed a mansion at the property's highest point, overlooking the Wissahickon and Whitemarsh Valleys. The siblings created a magnificent garden estate, complete with English park, oak allée, Japanese rock gardens, and fernery, which would become a public arboretum and school after their deaths. In the 1913 photograph above, laborers construct the Ravine Garden below the Mercury Loggia and Grotto, built by John Morris to celebrate the 25th anniversary of the founding of Compton. John died in 1915 and Lydia in 1932. After Lydia's death, Compton became the Morris Arboretum of the University of Pennsylvania, one of the country's leading horticultural research and teaching centers. Sadly, the Morris mansion was torn down in 1968. Shown below is its front hallway shortly before demolition.

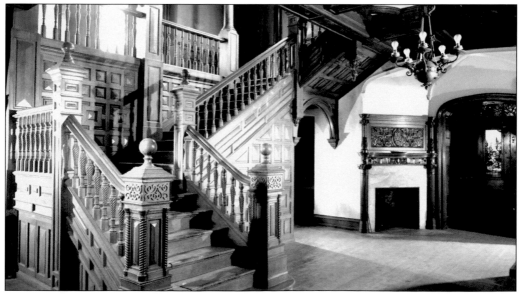

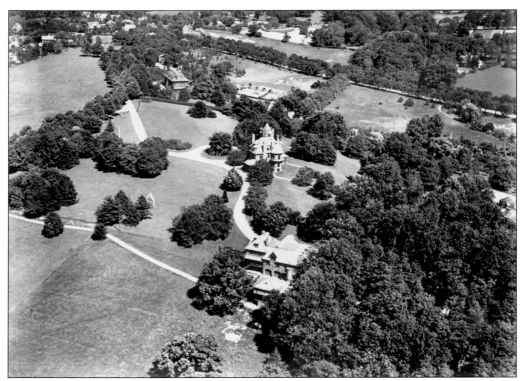

The Morris mansion is at the center of this 1920s aerial view of Compton. The carriage house at the bottom center was restored in 1982 and renamed the George D. Widener Education Center. Thomas Sovereign Gates Hall, in the upper left, was designed in 1893 by Wilson Eyre for David Pepper. It was bought by the University of Pennsylvania in 1948 as an administrative building for the arboretum. Hillcrest Avenue runs above the arboretum.

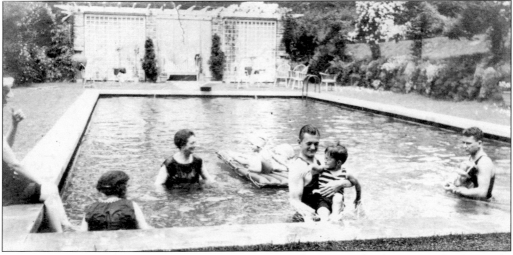

The Robert Glendinning family lived at 8862 Towanda Street, also known as the Squirrels. The mid-19th-century Italianate house with a terraced, multilevel garden overlooks the Wissahickon Valley. Glendinning, a noted aviator and balloonist, started a flying school at Essington in 1916 that became one of the government's first aviation academies during World War I. Here, the Glendinning family enjoys the pool at the Squirrels during the 1920s.

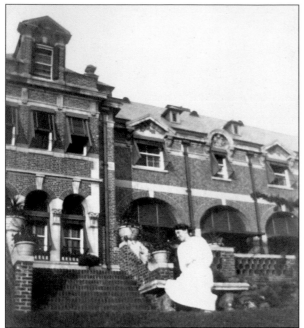

Kate's Hall, at 8440 St. Martin's Lane, was home to the Joseph Sill Clark family (whose chauffeur, George Cloverdale, appears on page 47). It was named for Clark's wife, Kate, who took an active role in designing the house with her architect cousin, Clarence C. Zantzinger. Built in 1902–1903, the house was radically altered in 1935 when part of the third floor was removed. In this early-20th-century photograph, two family members pose on the west side patio.

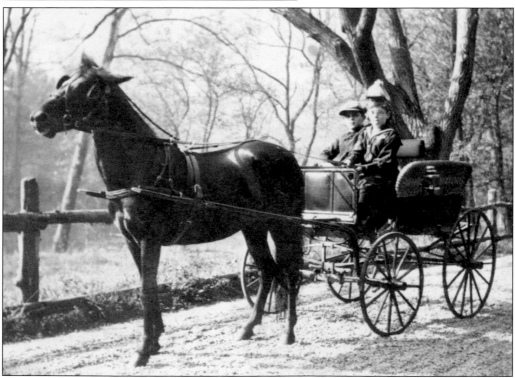

In 1952, Joseph S. Clark Jr. (left, with his brother Avery c. 1910) was elected the first Democratic mayor of Philadelphia in 67 years. As mayor, he oversaw the development of Penn Center and Society Hill. Clark went on to serve as U.S. senator from Pennsylvania from 1957 to 1969. As an adult, he lived at 440 Rex Avenue, created from two former servants' houses at Kate's Hall.

Five

THE HOUSTONS AND THE WOODWARDS

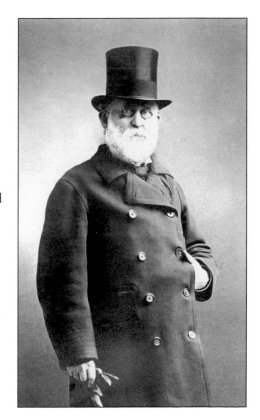

Born in York County in 1820, Henry Howard Houston worked in iron furnaces before joining the Pennsylvania Railroad in 1851. A master of planning and organization, Houston coordinated the deployment of Union troops and materiel during the Civil War. By the 1870s, he was a high-ranking railroad executive who multiplied his fortune through investments in oil, shipping, and real estate. Houston convinced the Pennsylvania Railroad to run a spur line through the west side of Germantown, Mount Airy, and Chestnut Hill in 1879. Eventually, he purchased 3,000 acres of farmland and forest in these areas, as well as in Roxborough and Montgomery County. With these raw materials in hand, Houston was ready to apply his managerial genius to the creation of a model suburb named Wissahickon Heights.

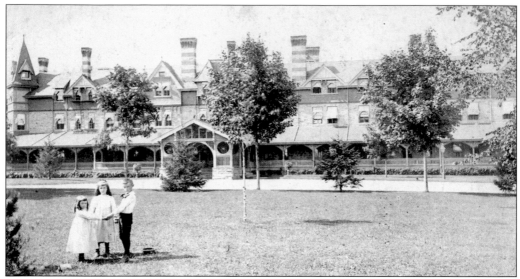

The first building planned by Houston was the Wissahickon Inn, a Queen Anne–style hotel designed by G.W. and W.D. Hewitt and built in 1883–1884 on the site of the Park Hotel. Visitors could hike through the Wissahickon Valley, stroll through St. Martin's Green arboretum, or canoe on Lake Surprise. By 1898, the inn's allure as a resort had faded, and Chestnut Hill Academy moved into the building. The inn closed completely in 1901.

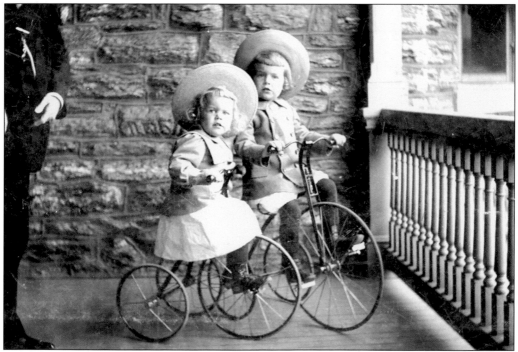

Houston saw the inn's guests not just as visitors but as potential residents in his suburb. Many guests, enchanted by Chestnut Hill's beauty, bought or rented houses nearby, often from Houston. William C. Melcher Jr. and Harold P. Melcher, shown here with their grandfather, stayed with their parents at the Wissahickon Inn in 1900 while waiting to move into their new house.

70

On June 11, 1884, the first train on the Philadelphia, Germantown, and Chestnut Hill Railroad line left Broad Street Station for Chestnut Hill, with Henry H. Houston as a passenger. It stopped at the Wissahickon Heights Station, then a one-story structure on West Willow Grove Avenue. A second story was added to the station in 1889. By the time this photograph was taken in the early 1900s, 32 trains traversed the line each day.

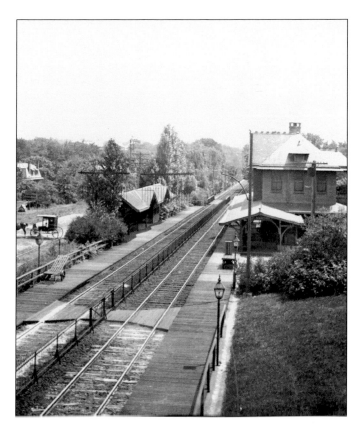

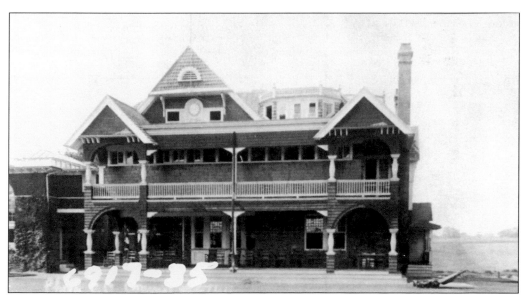

In 1884, Houston offered the homeless Philadelphia Cricket Club permanent grounds on West Willow Grove Avenue. The Hewitt-designed men's clubhouse opened October 1, 1884, with a cricket match, followed by an evening concert given by the Orpheus Club and a grand hop with music by Herzberg's Orchestra. This clubhouse burned in 1909 and was replaced the following year by the current Georgian Revival building designed by George T. Pearson.

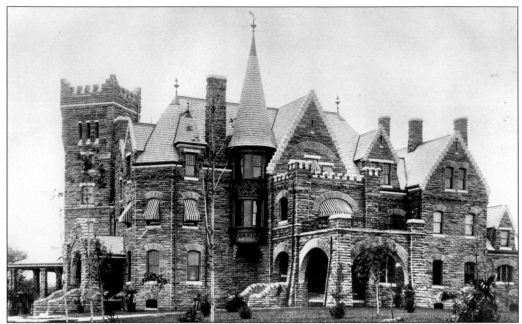

After completing the Wissahickon Inn, Houston turned to his own residence. Druim Moir (Gaelic for "great ridge") was designed by the Hewitts and built in 1885–1886 on Cherokee Street overlooking Fairmount Park. The 30-room Romanesque Revival mansion, dominated by a five-story square tower and a circular oriel, was the center of a 52-acre gentleman's estate with formal gardens, a working farm, and greenhouses. During World War II, Houston's son Samuel had the top floor and much of the tower removed. In 1957, the Springside School moved its Upper School to the front lawn, with the Lower School following in 1969. In 1980, the main house was subdivided into three residences, and other houses were built on the grounds. The photograph above shows Druim Moir shortly after its completion in 1886. The photograph below, taken from the roof, looks east over the front lawn where the Springside School is located today.

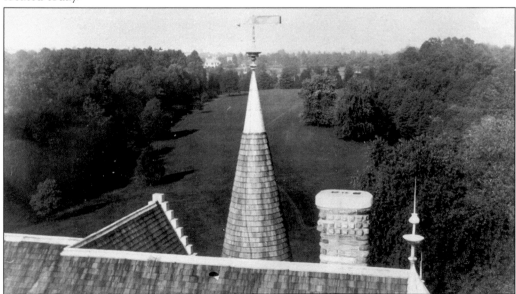

Henry H. Houston planned the Episcopal church of St. Martin-in-the-Fields as the spiritual center of Wissahickon Heights, paying for the Hewitts' design, the land, building, furnishings, and pastor's salary, at a cost of more than $100,000. Built in 1888–1889 at the northwest corner of Willow Grove Avenue and 31st Street, the church held its first service on February 2, 1889. In 1900, 31st Street was officially renamed St. Martin's Lane.

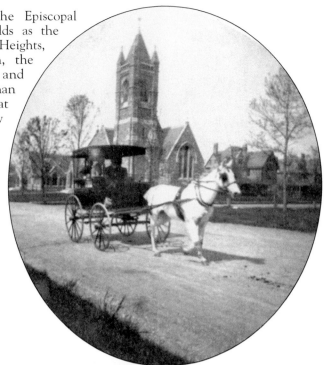

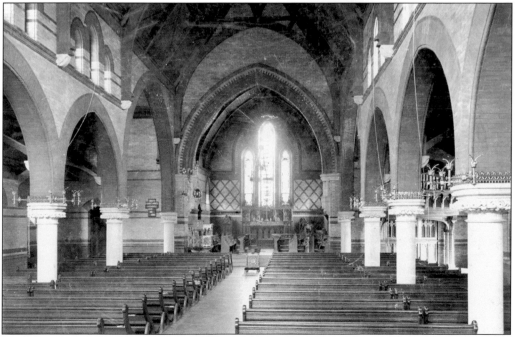

This photograph shows the interior of St. Martin-in-the-Fields, decorated in the high Victorian Gothic style popular in the late 19th century. In 1902, a Gothic chancel and sanctuary designed by Theophilus P. Chandler were added. The ornate metal fittings around the top of each pillar are gaslight fixtures. The church was completely restored by Philip Scott of Kise, Straw, & Kolodner in 2001. Today, the church interior closely resembles its original state.

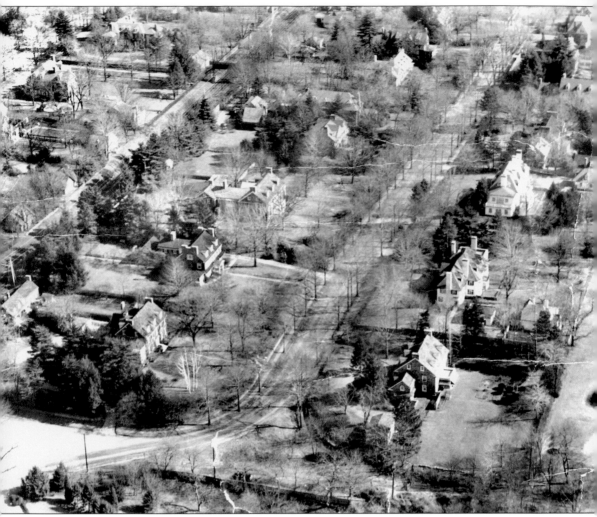

When Jacob LeRoy, first pastor of St. Martin-in-the-Fields, saw Wissahickon Heights in 1876, he described it as "unoccupied fields, covered with brush and bramble . . . forlorn and desolate." By the time of his death in 1895, Henry H. Houston had built roughly 100 houses at Wissahickon Heights. Some were sold, but most were rented to white, Protestant, upper-middle-class professionals and businessmen, who paid between $30 and $150 a month. In 1906, Houston's son-in-law George Woodward changed the train station name from Wissahickon Heights to St. Martin's, a name that spread to the entire neighborhood. During the same period, according to legend, Houston's daughter Gertrude Woodward gave the numbered streets the names of Native American tribes like Seminole, Cherokee, and Navajo. By the time this aerial view was taken *c.* 1925, St. Martin's had become one of Philadelphia's most attractive and affluent neighborhoods.

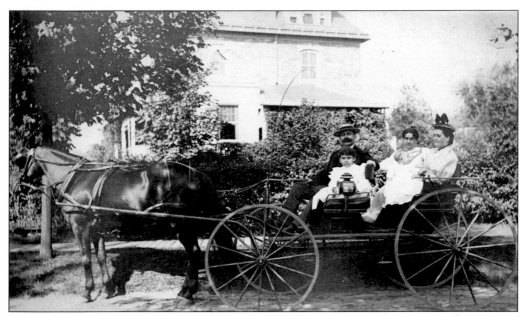

Houston built a number of single and semidetached houses in the Queen Anne and Second Empire styles in West Chestnut Hill. Although he rented most so that he could control the composition of the neighborhood as well as the condition of his properties, he sold some of the larger houses. One of these was 246 West Evergreen Avenue, sold in 1886 to Henry Bell, a shoe manufacturer whose family once owned the mill on Bell's Mill Road. The photograph above shows the Bells with their two daughters, Martha and May, and an unidentified woman in their carriage before their new home *c.* 1893. The photograph below, looking east toward Germantown Avenue, shows Mrs. Bell, Henry Jr., Martha, and the family kitten in the front yard. The Bell family would own 246 West Evergreen Avenue until 1955.

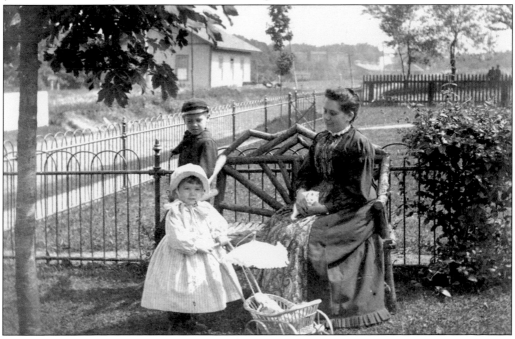

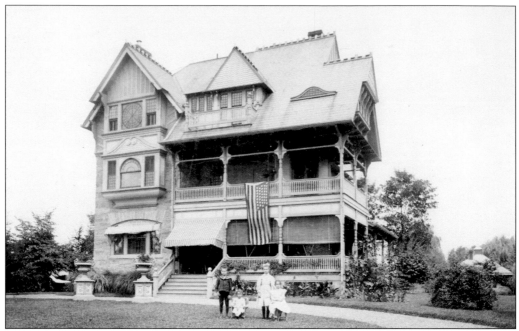

In 1889, Henry H. Houston sold 8205 Seminole Avenue to Louis C. Sauveur of the Provident Tradesman Bank & Trust Company. Louis died in 1894, but his wife, Ellen Lydia Sauveur, remained at the address until her death in 1961. Today, the Houston-Sauveur house is listed on the National Register of Historic Places as an outstanding example of the eclectic Queen Anne architectural style.

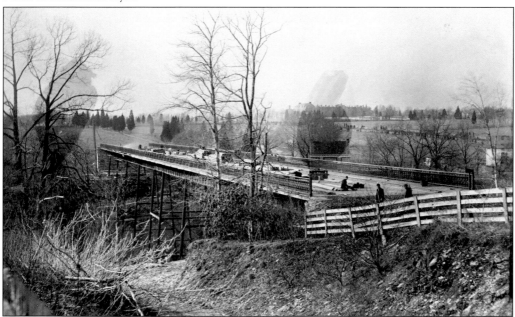

In July 1890, Henry H. Houston helped to underwrite the cost of a bridge that carried McCallum Street across the Cresheim Valley, connecting West Chestnut Hill and West Mount Airy in a continuous carriageway to Center City. Houston used the bridge to commute downtown from Druim Moir until the day he died in 1895.

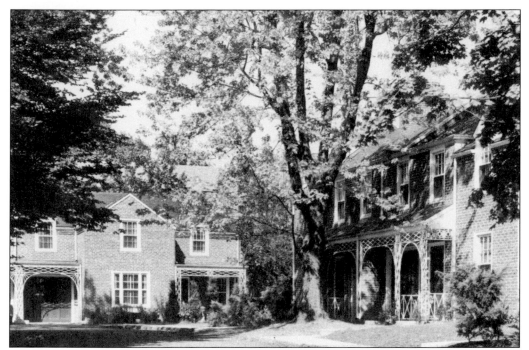

Henry H. Houston's son Samuel maintained and extended the Houston family holdings. Samuel hired Robert R. McGoodwin to create Tohopeka Court on West Highland Avenue. The complex featured brick twin houses framing a common courtyard. A tablet on a street wall reads, "O.S. 1845," marking the fact that Union Grove, the Owen Sheridan estate, stood on the site in the 1800s. Soon after, McGoodwin would design similar houses for another Samuel Houston development on Grakyn Lane in Upper Roxborough.

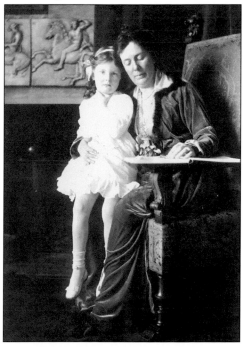

In 1916, Samuel Houston's second wife, Charlotte, and their daughter Eleanor pose for a portrait by Jessie Willcox Smith. This photographic study was taken by Smith, probably at her studio on St. George's Road. As an adult, Eleanor and her husband, L.M.C. Smith, became nationally known conservationists. With her six children and other Houston family members, Eleanor Houston Smith would be responsible for establishing two nature centers in northwest Philadelphia on Houston land: the Andorra Natural Area and the Schuylkill Center for Environmental Education.

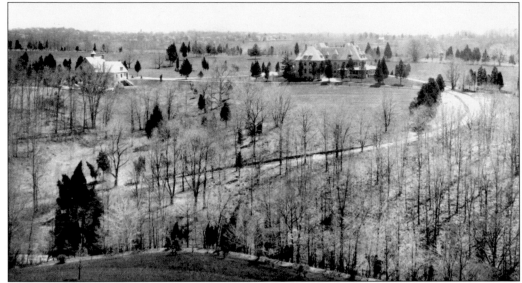

In 1887, Henry H. Houston gave 50 acres adjacent to Druim Moir as a present to his daughter Sallie upon her marriage to Charles Wolcott Henry. The Henrys named their estate Stonehurst, and hired the firm of McKim, Mead, & White to build a French château (shown above), with landscaping by the Olmsted Brothers. The estate was bordered by present-day Cherokee Street, Mermaid Lane, Valley Green Road, and the Wissahickon Valley. One of its notable features was a large outdoor swimming pool flanked by marble pillars (shown below), a popular summer spot for the Henry, Houston, and Woodward children. The château was demolished before World War II. In 1953, Mr. and Mrs. Donald D. Dodge (son-in-law and daughter of the Henrys) hired Oscar Stonorov to design Cherokee, a residential complex, on the Stonehurst site. The swimming pool survived until the late 1980s, when the lower part of the Cherokee site was developed.

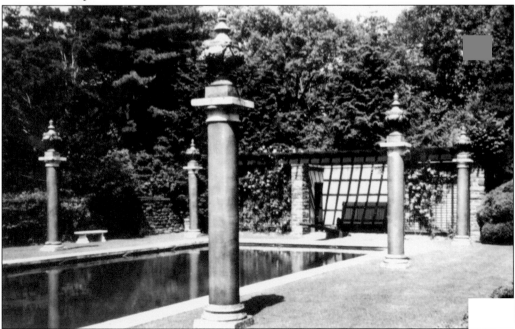

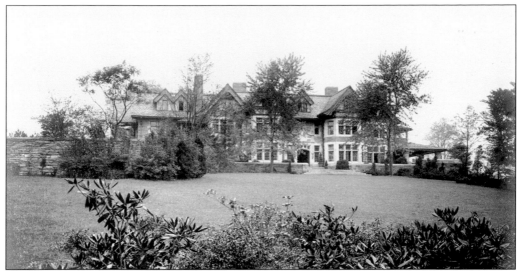

Krisheim, on McCallum Street near the Cresheim Valley, was the home of Henry H. Houston's daughter Gertrude and her husband, Progressive reformer Dr. George Woodward. The Woodwards hired the Boston firm of Peabody & Stearns to design a 30-room Elizabethan manor house, built between 1910 and 1912 (shown above). It featured a massive pipe organ that Leopold Stokowski would play once a week before he was named conductor of the Philadelphia Orchestra. Shown below is the Woodward family c. 1915 in the front entrance to Krisheim. Included in the photograph are, from left to right, George Woodward with his daughter Gertrude (nicknamed "Quita") on his lap, Stanley, Charles, George Jr., Henry, and Gertrude Houston Woodward. After Gertrude's death in 1961, Krisheim became a study center for the Presbyterian Church. In 1981, the Woodward family bought back the estate and returned it to residential use.

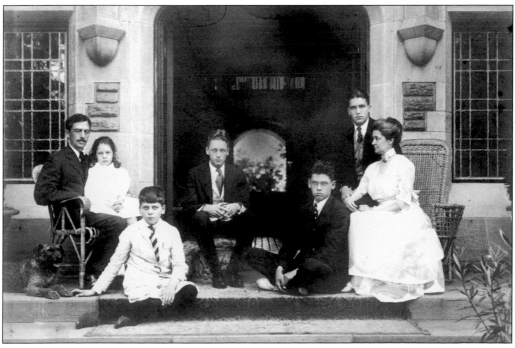

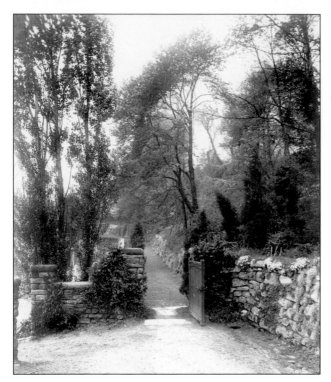

The Woodwards commissioned Frederick Dawson and the Olmsted Brothers to landscape the Krisheim site a decade before the house was built so that the building would rest in a mature setting. Krisheim is an outstanding example of the Wissahickon style of landscaping, which used water, stone, and native plants to create a microcosm of the nearby Wissahickon Valley. At Krisheim, formal gardens near the house gave way to a wilder, more natural area, which gradually merged into the forest below the house. This photograph shows the wall garden at Krisheim, a transitional passageway between the wild and formal areas of the gardens.

In 1906, the Woodwards persuaded artists Violet Oakley, Jessie Willcox Smith, and Elizabeth Shippen, along with their friend Henrietta Cozens, to move to West Mount Airy. Frank Miles Day remodeled a farmhouse for the four women, which they called Cogslea (their four initials, plus "lea" for valley). They named the street on which they lived St. George's Road after George Woodward. Violet Oakley remained at Cogslea until the 1960s. She created murals for the Pennsylvania State Capitol and the Chestnut Hill Academy Library in the Cogslea studio. On a 1928 trip to Italy, Oakley sketched the Woodwards' youngest child, Quita, who died of Hodgkin's disease in 1934 at age 25.

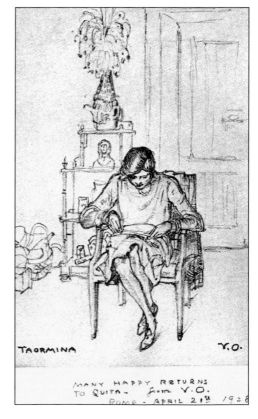

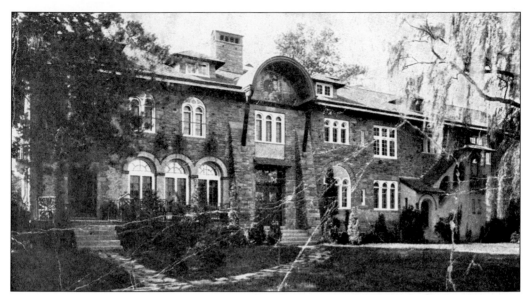

As part of their campaign to make Chestnut Hill a center for artists and craftsmen, the Woodwards persuaded William and Ann Willet to relocate their stained-glass studio from Pittsburgh in 1913. Duhring, Okie, & Ziegler converted Casey's Icehouse at 7902–06 Lincoln Drive (see page 51) into a studio and residence. The conversion was also part of the Woodwards' transformation of a rural area in West Chestnut Hill into a model suburb around Pastorius Park.

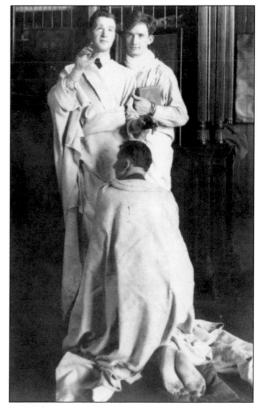

Henry Lee Willet, Richard Stewart, and an unidentified man pose for a stained-glass window for the Cadet's Chapel at West Point. Willet Studios created a window for this chapel every year from 1910 until 1976. The Willets stayed at Lincoln Drive until the early 1920s. After they left, the building was converted to apartments. Today, Willet Studios, a division of Hauser Art Glass, is located on East Moreland Avenue.

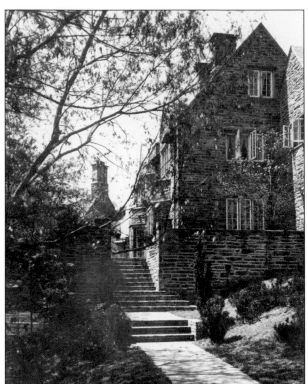

George and Gertrude Woodward built nearly 200 residences in Chestnut Hill and Mount Airy, ranging from Mermaid Lane mansions to Benezet Street quadruple houses. Their favorite architects—H. Louis Duhring, Edmund B. Gilchrist, and Robert R. McGoodwin—used different styles, layouts, and landscaping to give each project a unique appearance. McGoodwin's Cotswold Village adapted English country styles seen by the Woodwards on trips abroad. Like Henry H. Houston, the Woodwards rented rather than sold most of their houses, allowing them to control much of Chestnut Hill's population. Charles Woodward once joked about the rigorous screening of prospective tenants: "Often we'd find out that a woman was expecting a baby before her husband knew it!"

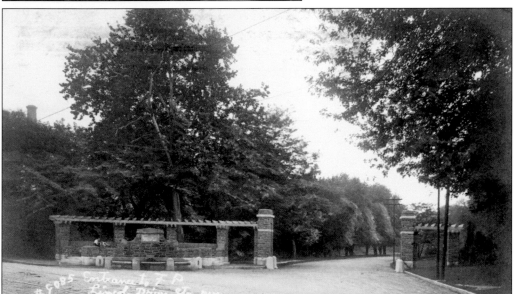

The Houston, Woodward, and Henry families strove to make Chestnut Hill the ideal garden suburb. In 1909, the Woodward and Henry families donated the pergola and watering trough at the intersection of Germantown Avenue and Cresheim Valley Road, as well as land to extend Fairmount Park along Cresheim Valley. The Woodwards were also heavily involved in the establishment of Pastorius Park, the Chestnut Hill Community Centre, and the Henry H. Houston Woodward Water Tower Recreation Center (given in memory of their oldest son, who died in World War I).

Six

CHESTNUT HILL
INSTITUTIONS

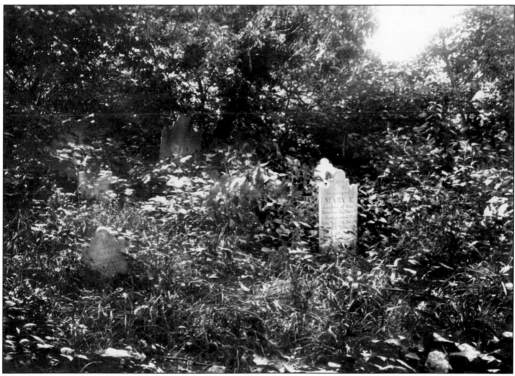

Chestnut Hill's first public cemetery, the Union Burying Ground, opened in 1828 on West Gravers Lane between Crefeld and Navajo Streets. By 1917, the derelict cemetery had been dubbed "No Man's Land" and was the scene of secret midnight burials. George Woodward bought it and had the remaining bodies moved to Arlington Cemetery in Upper Darby. Today, attractive stone houses cover the site. Nearby was the Union Chapel, which had been built in 1822 at the northwest corner of Gravers Lane and Shawnee Street and was shared by seven Protestant denominations. After each congregation opened its own church, the chapel was demolished c. 1890. (Courtesy Germantown Historical Society.)

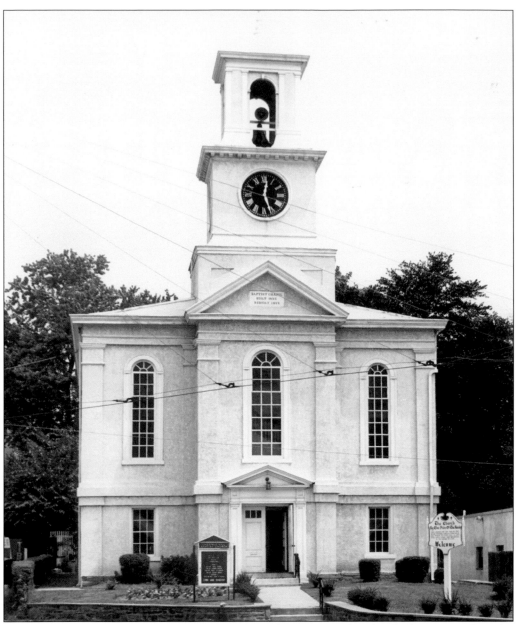

On May 23, 1835, the cornerstone was laid for the Baptist Church of Chestnut Hill at the southeast corner of Germantown Avenue and Bethlehem Pike. According to local legend, Washington and Lafayette met on the site to discuss strategy after the Battle of Germantown in 1777. Later, the land was used for a marble quarry and as the site of a traveling circus. The original 40- by 45-foot structure, the first single-denomination church built in Chestnut Hill, was enlarged in 1857. In 1874, a clock tower and bell were added. At the time, the Presbyterians were considering adding a clock to their nearby steeple. When the Baptists built theirs first, the Presbyterians concluded that a second one would be superfluous and resigned themselves to going to church on "Baptist time." In 1974, "the Church by the Side of the Road" was declared a historic building by the Philadelphia Historical Commission. (Courtesy Germantown Historical Society.)

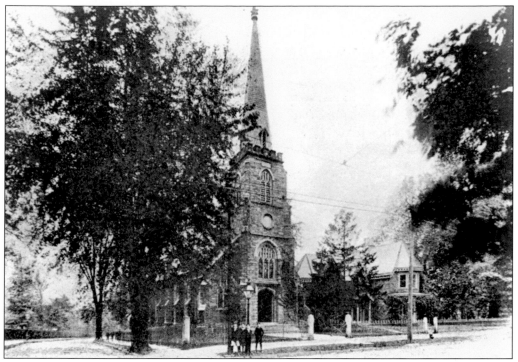

The Presbyterian Church of Chestnut Hill was designed by John Notman and built in 1852–1853 at the northwest corner of Germantown and Rex Avenues. The church moved to a new building at 8855 Germantown Avenue in 1949. Its original building (minus its steeple, removed in 1948) serves today as the Seventh-day Adventist Church. The rectory, seen to the right, has housed the Chestnut Hill Historical Society since 1985.

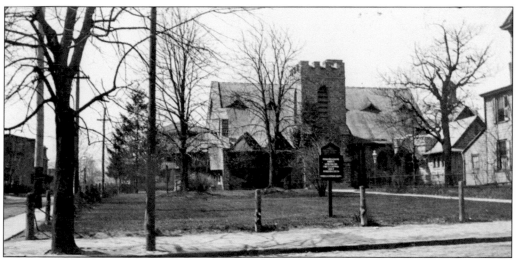

In 1889, a schism among parishioners at the Presbyterian Church resulted in the formation of Trinity Presbyterian Church (see page 42). A chapel was built at the northwest corner of Germantown Avenue and Gravers Lane, leaving the front lot open for a larger church that was never constructed. In December 1929, the two churches voted to reunite, and Trinity was demolished. The Shoppes of Chestnut Hill were built on the site in 1992.

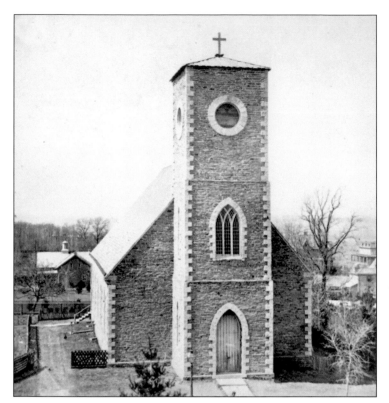

Joseph Middleton, a wealthy convert to Catholicism, oversaw the creation of a Catholic church in Chestnut Hill despite the resistance of Protestant neighbors. St. Mary's Lady of Consolation Church (known today as Our Mother of Consolation) was built on East Chestnut Hill Avenue in 1855. This 1860s stereopticon slide shows the church's original steeple, replaced by a tall Gothic spire in 1885. The current spire dates from the 1950s.

In 1856, the newly organized St. Paul's Episcopal Church erected a stone chapel across from the Catholic church. This 1866 stereopticon slide shows the chapel on the left and a larger church built in 1861, as well as the Italianate villas on Summit Avenue behind the church. In 1929, Zantzinger, Borie, & Medary designed the present church, parish house, and Sunday school. The 1856 chapel now serves as St. Paul's auditorium.

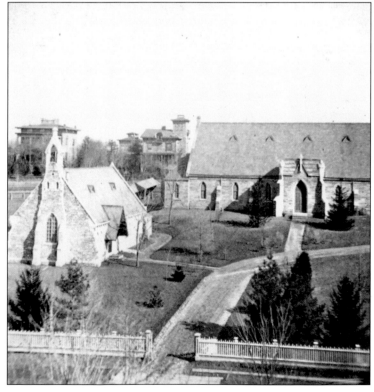

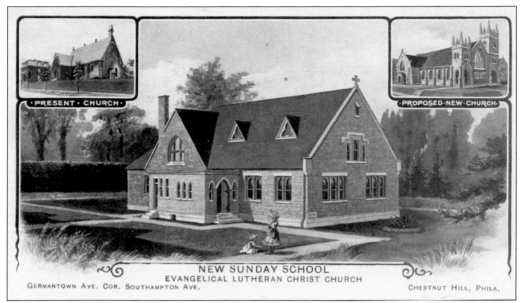

In June 1871, the Christ Evangelical Lutheran Church (now Christ-Ascension) was consecrated at the northwest corner of Germantown and Southampton Avenues. Three months later, the chapel bell from the demolished Mower Hospital (see page 30) was placed in its belfry, where it hangs today. This *c.* 1910 postcard shows the new Sunday school building, the present church in the upper left, and a never-executed Gothic redesign in the upper right.

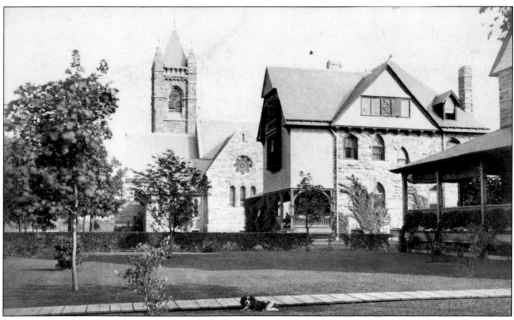

Henry H. Houston created the Episcopal Church of St. Martin-in-the-Fields as the anchor of his planned suburb, Wissahickon Heights (see page 73). Designed by G.W. and W.D. Hewitt, the church was erected in 1888–1889 at the corner of Willow Grove Avenue and 31st Street (later renamed St. Martin's Lane). This photograph, taken *c.* 1900, shows the original rectory, Hilary House (8020 St. Martin's Lane), also designed by the Hewitt Brothers.

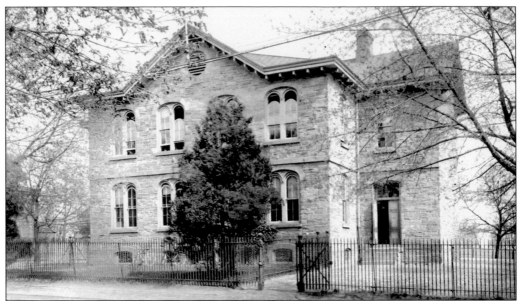

The Harmony School, Chestnut Hill's first public school, was founded in 1794. Named Harmony because it accepted students from both Philadelphia and Springfield Township, it was located first on Bethlehem Pike, then at Highland Avenue and Shawnee Street. In 1871, the city built the Chestnut Hill Consolidated School (shown above) at 212 West Highland Avenue. It was renamed the Josephus C. Gilbert School in 1896 after a local physician and politician who donated the land for the school. The school closed in 1924, when the John Story Jenks School was completed, and was replaced by apartments. The photograph below shows Gilbert School students dressed for a patriotic pageant in the Germantown High School gym in 1916. Some of the students pictured include Marion Barnes, Arthur Conway, Jean Dunn, J. Gerson, Radcliffe Heberton, and Charles Roth.

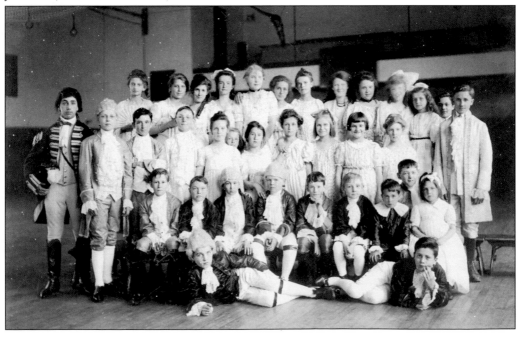

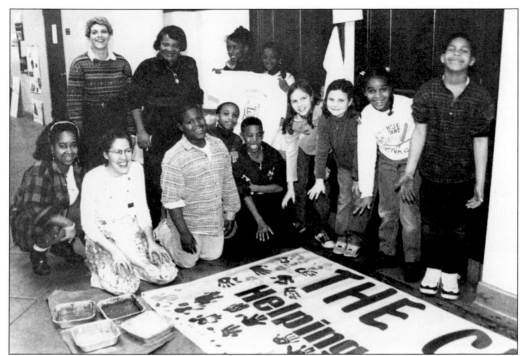

The John Story Jenks Elementary School was built at Germantown and Southampton Avenues in 1924. Its namesake, John Story Jenks, was a wealthy merchant and Civil War veteran who lived at Inglewood on Bethlehem Pike (see page 25). Today, about 600 students attend kindergarten through eighth grade there. In this 1997 photograph, Jenks students, teachers, and parents place their handprints on a banner promoting the children's park and playground built on the school grounds that year.

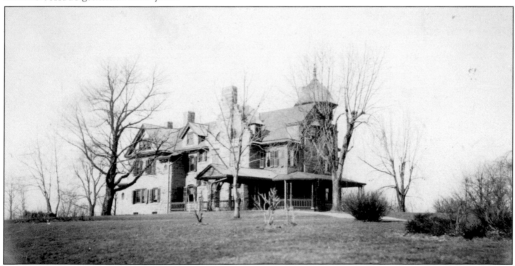

The Stevens School was founded in 1868 as a girls' school in Germantown. In 1935, it took over the Shady Hill School in Chestnut Hill as a junior school. In 1953, the entire school relocated to Highfield, the George V. Rex House at 8836 Crefeld Street. The Stevens School moved back to Germantown in 1974 and closed in 1982. Today, the Crefeld School, a coeducational day school, occupies the Crefeld Street campus.

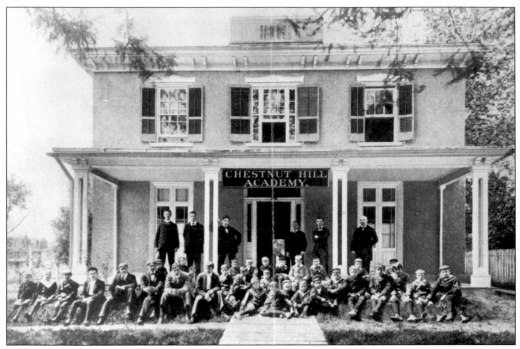

The Chestnut Hill Academy for boys was founded in 1850 by brothers Joshua T. Owen and Roger Owen, D.D., at the southwest corner of Germantown and Springfield Avenues. Shortly after, Roger became first pastor of the Chestnut Hill Presbyterian Church, while Joshua rose to the rank of brigadier general during the Civil War. After the Owens's departure, the academy stagnated until it was reorganized in 1895 at 8030 Germantown Avenue (shown above). In 1898, the academy moved to the Wissahickon Inn, taking over the building when the inn closed in 1901 (see page 70). St. Martin's Green, a promenade for inn guests, became the academy playing field. The photograph below shows academy students c. 1910, at St. Martin's Green with St. Martin-in-the-Fields in the background. After the academy moved, 8030 Germantown Avenue was purchased by the Venetian Club and remodeled as its clubhouse.

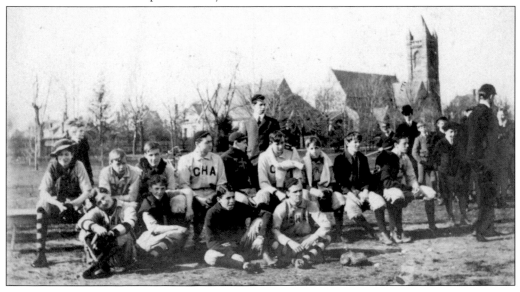

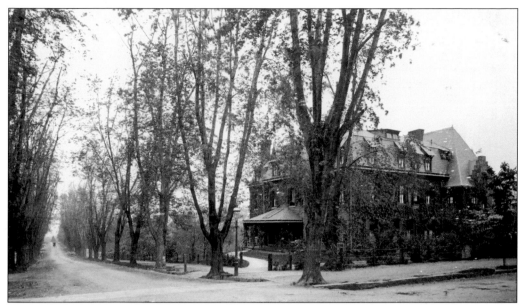

The oldest extant girls' school in Philadelphia was founded in 1879 by Mrs. Walter D. Comegys and Jane Bell as "the French and English Boarding and Day School for Young Ladies and Little Girls." First located on Summit Street, the school moved to the Justus Donat farm in 1881 and was renamed Springside in 1901 after a nearby spring. The photograph above shows the main building in 1885 at the northwest corner of Norwood and East Chestnut Hill Avenues, looking down Norwood. The photograph below shows Springside students in 1916 rehearsing a dance on the tennis courts, perhaps for a school pageant. In 1957, the school moved to a new campus on the front lawn of Druim Moir, the Henry H. Houston estate. The Norwood Avenue building was demolished *c.* 1963 and replaced by doctors' offices and a parking lot.

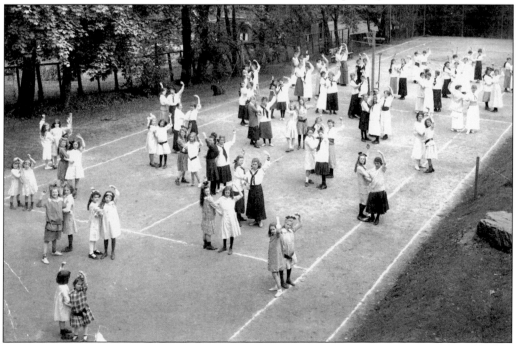

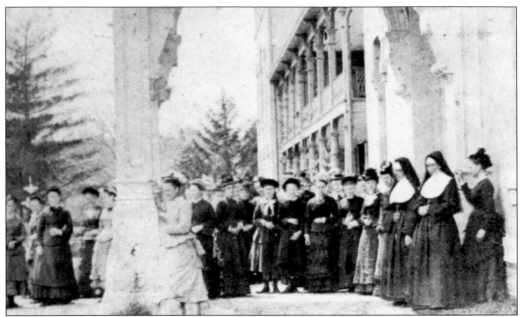

In 1858, the Order of the Sisters of St. Joseph established a Catholic convent and girls' seminary at Monticello, the Joseph Middleton estate at Germantown and Northwestern Avenues. On August 22, 1874, the cornerstone was laid for the Mount St. Joseph Female Academy building. Shown second from right is Sister Clement, later Mother Clement, superior general of the Sisters of St. Joseph. A college was founded on the site in 1924 and renamed Chestnut Hill College in 1938.

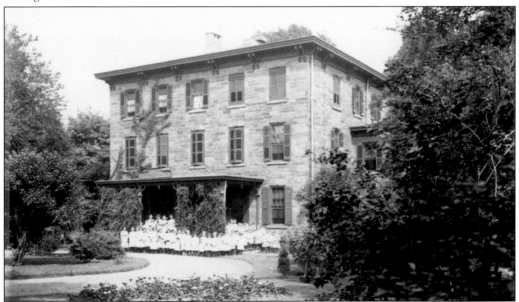

The Bethesda Home housed orphans and needy children from 1859 until 1950. The home was lodged in the Park Hotel (predecessor to the Wissahickon Inn) and 8419 Germantown Avenue (later the community center) before moving to the southeast corner of Stenton and Willow Grove Avenues in 1872. After the home closed in 1950, the building shown above was demolished and replaced by private homes.

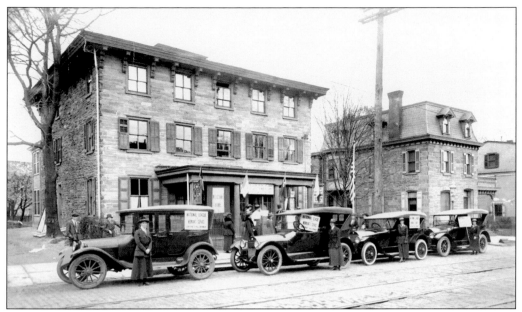

During World War I, the Chestnut Hill Branch of the National League for Women's Service purchased 8419 Germantown Avenue. This photograph shows the League's Motor Brigade in front of its headquarters in 1918. After the war, a community center was founded that worked to improve substandard housing and conducted Americanization classes among immigrants. Today, the center houses the Bird in Hand Consignment Shop, the Happy Butterfly, and the Chestnut Hill Women's Exchange.

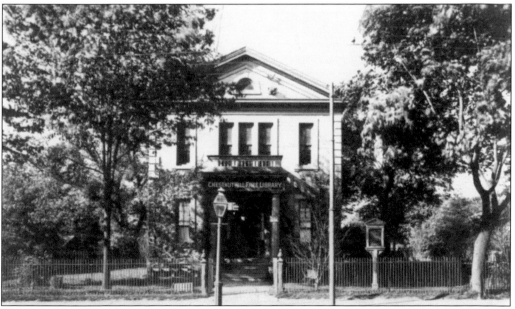

Christian Hall Library was founded in 1871 at 8711 Germantown Avenue by Henry J. Williams. He included Christian in the library's name because he did not wish any meetings held there "inconsistent with the word 'Christian.'" In 1897, the Free Library of Philadelphia (organized 1891) took over Christian Hall Library. The building shown here was replaced in 1907 by the present Free Library branch, designed by Cope & Stewardson.

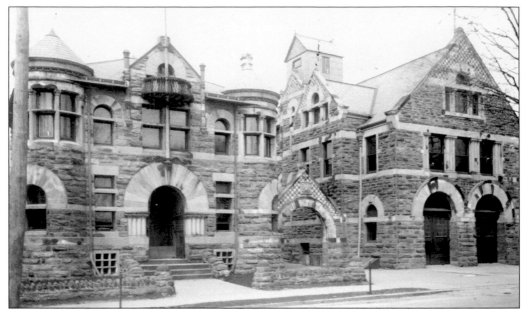

The Chestnut Hill police substation and firehouse were erected between 1892 and 1894 on the former site of the Harmony School on West Highland Avenue above Shawnee Street. This *c.* 1910 postcard shows the police substation on the left and the firehouse on the right. In 1949, the 14th district in Germantown became police headquarters for Chestnut Hill. The abandoned Highland Avenue substation was demolished in 1959 after 10 years of neglect.

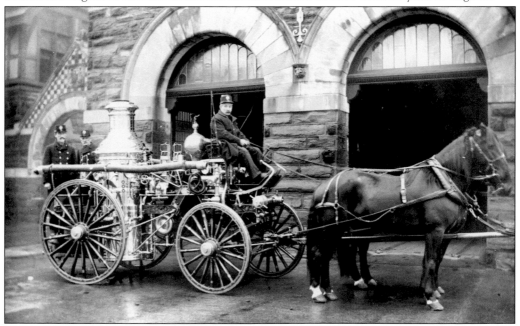

The Congress Fire Company, Chestnut Hill's first volunteer company, existed from 1816 until 1871, when Philadelphia established a municipal fire department. Engine Company 37 was organized in 1891 and, in 1894, moved into the Highland Avenue Firehouse, where it is still stationed. This *c.* 1900 photograph shows the company's horse-drawn Silsby Rotary Steamer. The last fire horse retired in 1916, replaced by a Mack combination hose and chemical wagon.

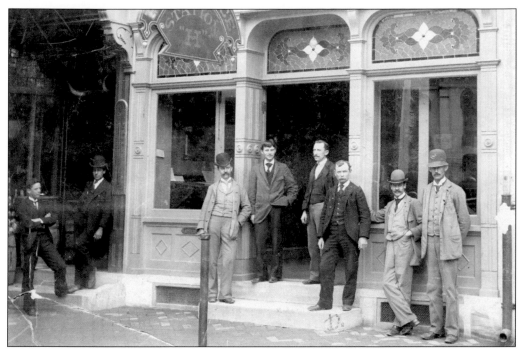

The first Chestnut Hill post office was established in 1828 at the tollgate at Germantown Avenue and East Evergreen Avenue, with gatekeeper Jacob Guyer as postmaster. The photograph above shows Post Office Station H at 8622 Germantown Avenue *c.* 1895, with postmaster Walter A. Dwyer Sr. (third from the right) and police officer Edward Connors (far right). Well into the 20th century, many Chestnut Hill residents received their mail deliveries via horse. The photograph below shows Mr. Lazelere, one of three local carriers, in front of the post office in Joslin Hall, at 8434 Germantown Avenue, *c.* 1910. In 1923, the post office moved to a building at 10–12 West Gravers Lane, behind the Chestnut Hill Title and Trust Company. Today, Chestnut Hill is served by post offices at Germantown Avenue and Market Square.

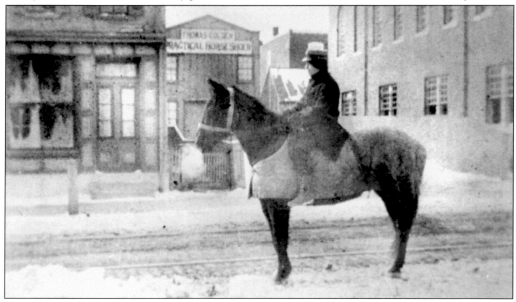

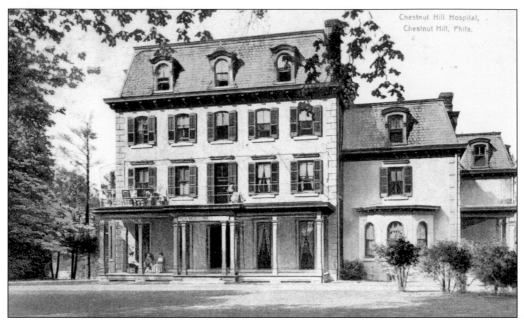

The Chestnut Hill Hospital, chartered in November 1903, officially opened on October 4, 1904, in two houses at 27 and 29 West Gravers Lane. Its seven founders and trustees included physicians Radcliffe Cheston, the first president, and John F. McCloskey. In 1907, the trustees bought Norrington, the Norris estate at 8815 Germantown Avenue, and converted it to a hospital. In 1921–1922, a new medical building was constructed and Norrington was converted to a maternity ward. The *c.* 1910 postcard above shows Norrington, which was demolished in 1980. The *c.* 1920 photograph below shows McCloskey (second from the right) and staff in a Norrington operating room. "Dr. John," as he was known, was still on the hospital's staff in 1951 and also served as team physician for the Philadelphia Eagles.

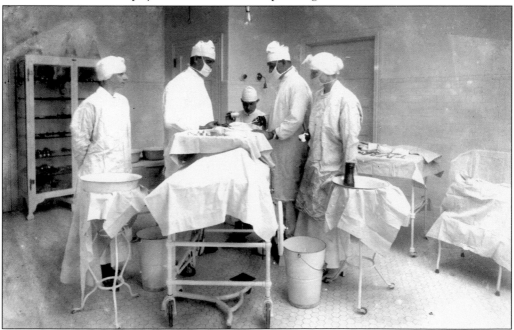

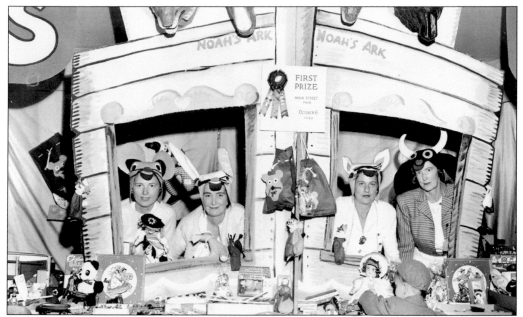

In 1943, the Chestnut Hill Hospital Ladies' Auxiliary held the first Main Street Fair, raising $3,000 for the hospital. For the next four decades, the Main Street Fair was an annual event, with carnival rides, games, and rummage sales. These imaginatively topped ladies, whose booth won first prize in 1948, are, from left to right, Mrs. Walter M. Schwartz Jr., Mrs. H.P. Glendinning, Mrs. Flagler Harris, and Mrs. H. Martyn Kneedler.

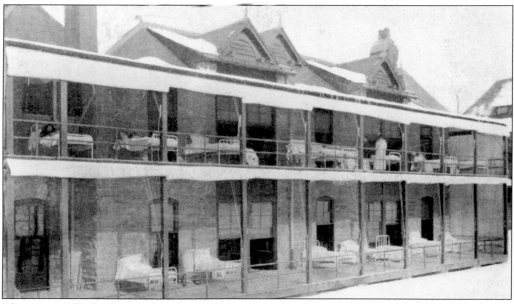

Chestnut Hill's healthy atmosphere made it popular for invalids, including "consumptives" (tuberculosis patients). In 1885, William Bucknell donated his estate at 8601 Stenton Avenue to the Philadelphia Protestant Episcopal Mission Home for Consumptives, also known as All Saints' Hospital. This c. 1900 photograph shows patients' outdoor sleeping porches on the Wilstach Cottage, designed by Frank Furness. Today, All Saints' is known as the Chestnut Hill Rehabilitation Hospital.

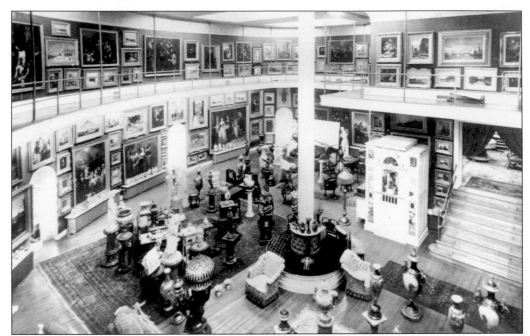

Charles Knox Smith bequeathed his residence, Woodmere (see pages 24 and 64), and his art collection as a public museum and gallery after his death in 1916. Due to family residency and legal challenges by other Philadelphia museums, the Woodmere Gallery did not open until 1940. Today, the Woodmere Art Museum is a leading regional museum. The photograph shows the current Catherine M. Kuch Gallery as it appeared after Smith's death.

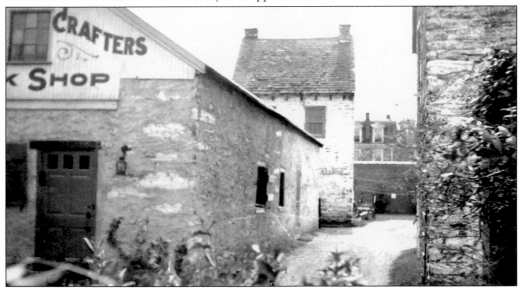

The Stagecrafters Community Theater was organized in 1929 by members of the Germantown Women's Club, who rented 8130 Germantown Avenue as a workshop for theatrical scenery (shown above). The house in the rear was rented as a theater in 1931. In 1936, both structures were absorbed by a new theater. The Stagecrafters purchased the 1753 Peters House at 8134 Germantown Avenue, on the right, as their office. Today, the theater presents six productions a year.

Seven

LEISURE

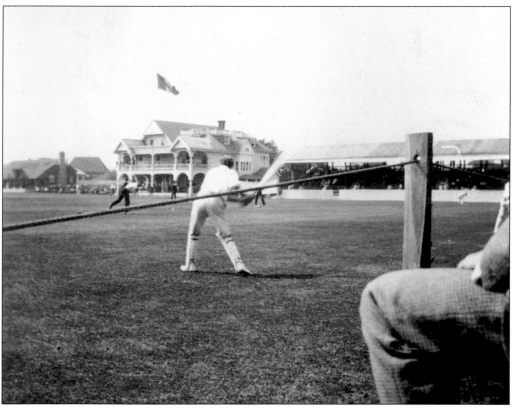

Chestnut Hill first became a destination for leisure activities because of its elevation, cool breezes, countryside, and the natural beauty of the Wissahickon gorge. English hosiery weavers living in Germantown during the 1840s brought cricket to America. A group of young Philadelphians formed the Philadelphia Cricket Club in 1854 and played on several fields in the Philadelphia area, including one at Chestnut Hill Avenue and Crefeld Street and another along Bethlehem Pike above the Eldon Hotel. In 1884, Henry H. Houston gave land on West Willow Grove Avenue for the Philadelphia Cricket Club (see page 71), shown here in 1899. The Philadelphia Cricket Club is the nation's oldest country club still in existence. The original charter states that its object was the "practicing and playing the games of cricket and tennis and the promotion of the health of the members." (Courtesy Germantown Historical Society.)

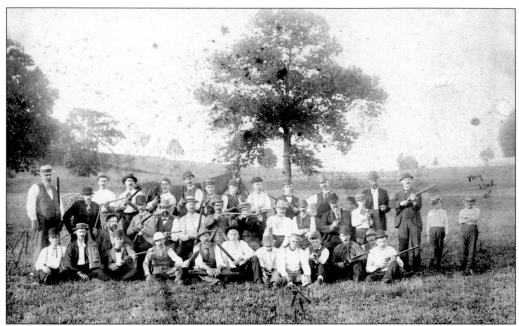

In 1861, this Chestnut Hill group assembled for a shooting party, including John Landis (left), Will Detweiler Sr. (seated fifth from right), and 12-year-old Will Lewis Detweiler Jr. (far right).

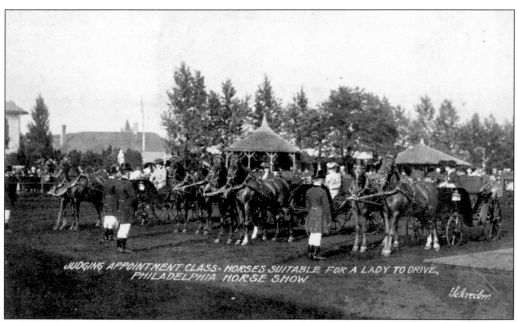

In the spring of 1892, the first Philadelphia Horse Show was held east of the Wissahickon Inn between Springfield and Willow Grove Avenues. It became so popular by 1895 that its grounds expanded across Willow Grove Avenue to where the Chestnut Hill Academy playing fields and tennis courts are today. That year, 10,000 visitors came. There were stables, a grandstand, and a clubhouse with a restaurant. After a fire razed some of the buildings, new ones were built. Eventually, neighbors complained about the large number of combustible wood-frame buildings, and after 1908 the horse show moved to the Main Line to become the Devon Horse Show.

The Philadelphia Lawn Tennis Women's champions of 1885 (right) were Mrs. Harry Toulman, Mrs. William Stewart, Mrs. Bradford Knight, and Mrs. Taylor Allerdice. Tennis was popular with the affluent residents who formed the Chestnut Hill Tennis Club in the early 1880s, which shared courts at the Philadelphia Cricket Club beginning in 1884. In 1889, they opened their own courts on Bethlehem Pike near Stenton Avenue on what is now the uphill end of the Fairview Care Center property. The Chestnut Hill Tennis Club, still in existence in the 1920s, soon merged with the Philadelphia Cricket Club. Elsie Little, Edith Rotch, and Natalie Wildey demonstrate their athleticism despite their long skirts at the Women's National Tennis Tournament at the Philadelphia Cricket Club in 1908 (below).

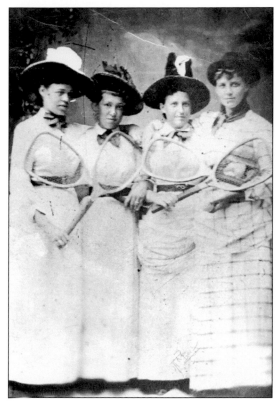

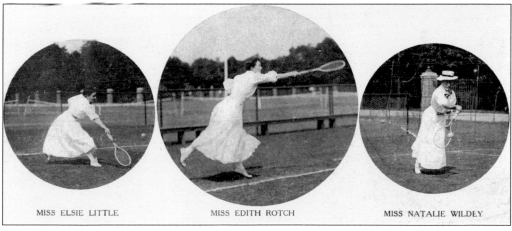

MISS ELSIE LITTLE   MISS EDITH ROTCH   MISS NATALIE WILDEY

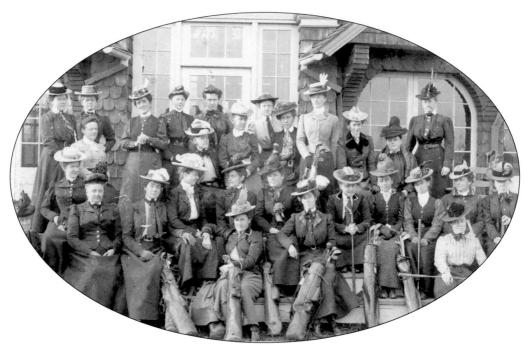

As cricket began to wane in popularity c. 1900, golf gained a large following with the opening of the Philadelphia Cricket Club's new golf course at Wissahickon Heights in 1896. Ladies' golf teams existed as early as 1898, about the date of this photograph of a group of golfers relaxing in front of one of the early Queen Anne–style buildings at the Philadelphia Cricket Club. Squash racquets and soccer were introduced at the club in 1902, and baseball in 1910.

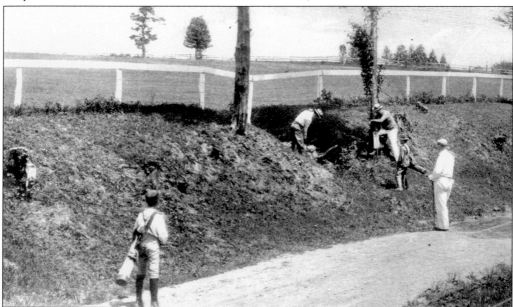

A golfer in October 1897 tries to hit his way out of a tough situation along West Hartwell Lane on the first fairway of the St. Martin's golf course, as two youthful caddies look on. The Cricket Club hosted the U.S. Golf Association Open Championships in 1907 and 1910. Jack Hobens made the first hole-in-one at a U.S. Open here in 1907.

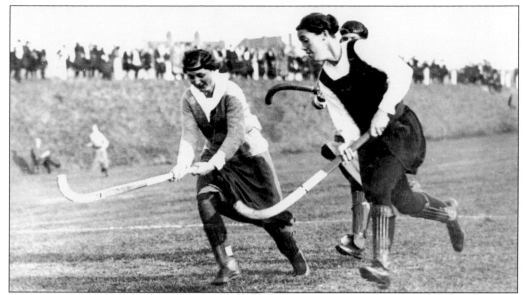

A women's field hockey team, one of the first in this country, was formed at the Philadelphia Cricket Club in 1903. At that time, skirts had to be six inches from the ground. The team won 11 national championships in a row. The Philadelphia Cricket Club organized a Philadelphia team, with nine out of the 15 players hailing from Chestnut Hill, to challenge a British team in 1920. Pictured on the left is Ella Read Brewster, Cricket Club member, scrambling to beat her British opponent on an English field.

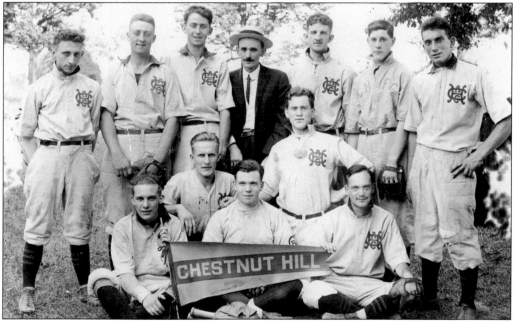

With the prohibition of alcoholic beverages in 1919, saloons went out of business, and their patrons sought other places to gather for a drink. Attendance grew at twilight baseball games played by local amateur teams. Dan Higgins (back row, third from the left) was born in 1895 in Chestnut Hill. He managed the Chestnut Hill Athletic Club baseball team, pictured here c. 1920, which often played at the Water Tower Recreation Center field.

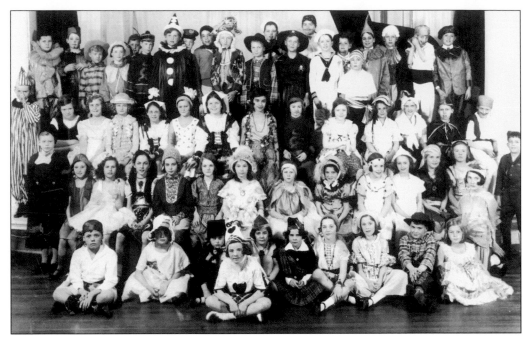

Starting around third grade, children of well-to-do Chestnut Hill families were invited to afternoon dance classes at the Philadelphia Cricket Club. Here, the Monday afternoon class poses in elaborate costumes in 1931. The boy in the clown suit on the left is not amused and sucks his thumb. At about age 15, the children's venue changed to the Bellevue-Stratford or Warwick Hotels downtown on weekend evenings, where young Chestnut Hillers could meet their social peers from the Main Line and other areas. This culminated in a round of debutante parties when a girl became 18.

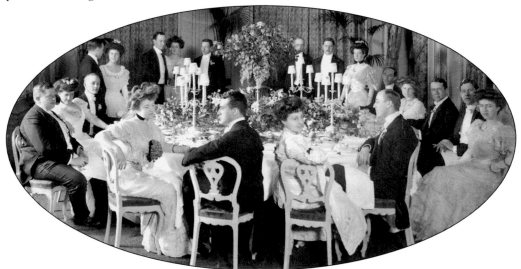

The Bellevue-Stratford Hotel was the setting for this party, whose Chestnut Hill guests included Carroll Tyson Sr. (with the moustache), his daughter Maggie Tyson Bond (third woman from the left), and other family members. The other guests are the Ingersolls and Lippincotts. Working-class families attended dances at the Venetian Club and the second floor of Joslin Hall.

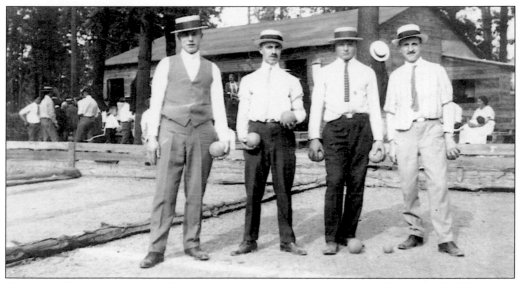

Venetian Club members, mostly northern Italian immigrants, originally met at the Marcolina Quarry in nearby Laverock, pictured here in the early 1920s. Dante Colussi, right, plays bocce with friends on a Sunday afternoon. Colussi was a tile setter who immigrated at age 32 in 1920 from Poffabro, north of Venice, as did some 200 Chestnut Hill families. At home, the Marcolina and Colussi families spoke Italian. Colussi's niece, born in Chestnut Hill in the 1930s, amused the townspeople of Poffabro when she visited in 1990 because she spoke an antiquated form of their dialect that only the old people remembered. (Courtesy Germantown Historical Society.)

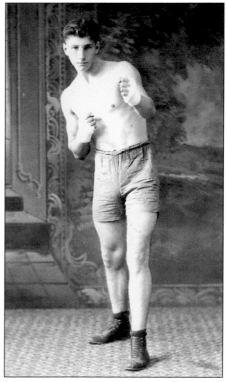

Semiprofessional boxer Richard Roman immigrated from Poffabro and later ran a business as a terrazzo and tile setter. Roman was a member of the Venetian Club, whose members took great pride in his boxing successes. The Venetian Club bought a building at 8030 Germantown Avenue (see page 90) to use as a clubhouse and in 1930 added the façade visible today. Club membership was by invitation only, although non-Italian neighbors were welcome at their dances. Three generations could be found enjoying an evening together, dancing to music provided by the members. Southern Italians in Chestnut Hill founded the Bocce Club at the southwest corner of East Hartwell Land and Devon Street. (Courtesy Germantown Historical Society.)

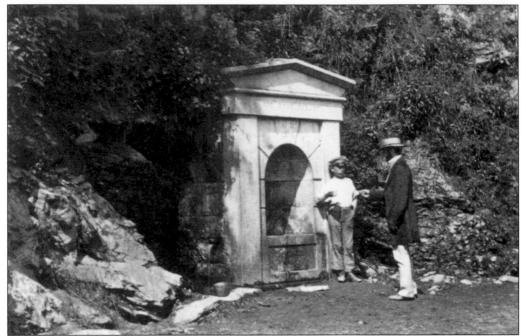

John Moran took this *c.* 1858 photograph of the public drinking fountain built in 1854 near a spring along the Wissahickon Creek by the Rex Avenue bridge. John Cooke, brother-in-law of landowner Joseph Middleton, designed and donated this amenity, which reads, "PRO BONO PUBLICO ESTO PERPETUA," meaning "for the public good, may it be forever." The fountain stands today, but the city disconnected the fountain in the 1950s for fear of unclean drinking water.

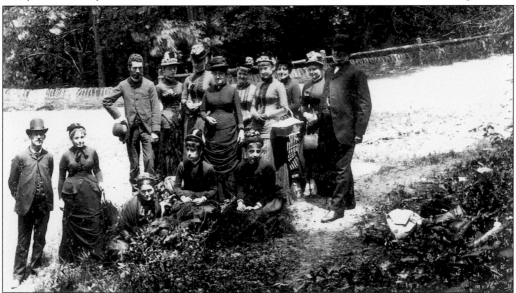

A musical club is gathered on the east end of the bridge over the Wissahickon Creek at Springfield Avenue en route to their picnic in the 1880s. Jane Campbell of Germantown, a leader in the women's suffrage movement, standing in the front center, compiled more than 100 scrapbooks with photographs of Philadelphia. Her photograph collection contains the only known images of many buildings, now demolished, including several shown in this book.

The Lenape tribe of Native Americans was said to have gathered on Council Rock below what is now Rex Avenue, on a promontory above the Wissahickon. The Lenape moved northward out of the area after the treaty with William Penn in 1682. In 1856, five men, including Joseph Middleton, placed a large painted wood panel of a standing Native American on this rock. Effects of weather ravaged the original wood panel and then this replacement until it was removed in 1902. (Courtesy Germantown Historical Society.)

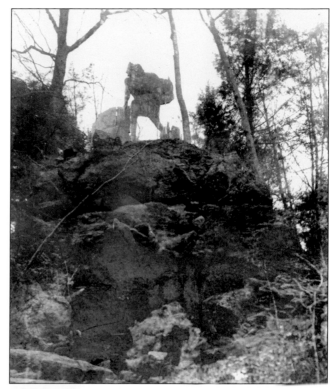

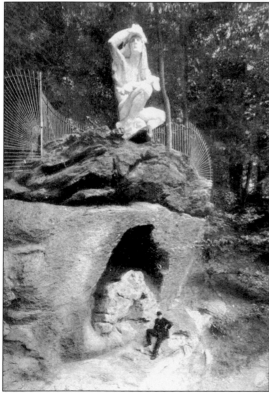

Charles W. Henry and his wife, Sallie Houston Henry, replaced the deteriorating wooden Native American panel with a marble statue of a kneeling Native American in 1902. This idealized figure of a Native American by John Massey Rhind represented Lenape chief Tedyuscung, according to 1902 newspaper reports of the dedication ceremonies. Indian Rock has been a destination for hikers hardy enough to walk up the steep hill.

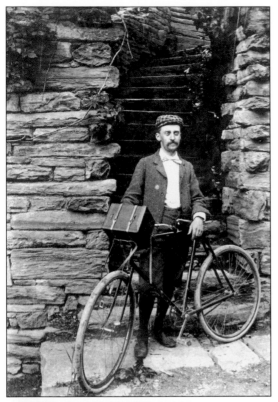

Around 1890, safety bikes like this one began to take the place of high-wheeled bicycles. Bicycle clubs grew in popularity, featuring bicycle shows and "hare-and-hound chases." In 1896, amateur photographer James Rich, wife Sarah, and daughter Hazel enjoyed biking along the Wissahickon Creek, with James taking their pictures. James has his camera box strapped to the handlebars of his bike. The stone arch beside the Rex Avenue bridge led up the steps to Indian Rock. The rusticated arch shown in this photograph was later rebuilt with rounded stone buttresses.

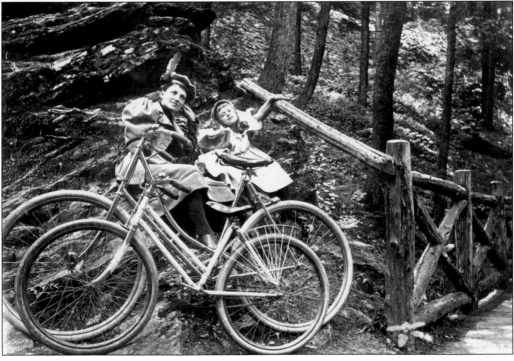

In 1899, James Rich photographed his daughter Hazel (right) and others enjoying boating on the Wissahickon Creek. The creek level was more uniformly high before the city expanded in the 20th century. Impervious streets and buildings reduced groundwater levels, lowering the creek, and at the same time increased storm water runoff, causing periods of flooding.

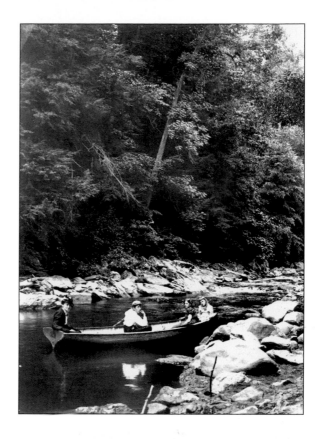

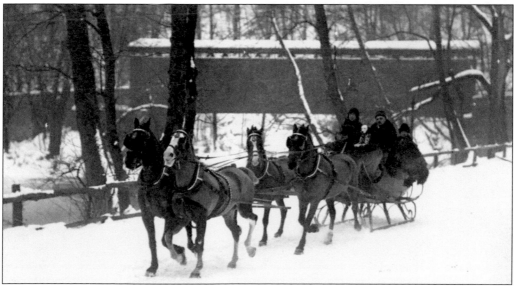

This scene along the Wissahickon Creek near Thomas Mill Road was part of a 1938 Christmas card from the Price family, who lived at 139 Bethlehem Pike. When Bethlehem Pike became a paved road, John Sergeant Price Jr. (center) was instrumental in having the Northwestern Avenue stables built, where he and others could keep their horses. His niece Gwen Martin is driving the sleigh with a Dalmatian dog beside her.

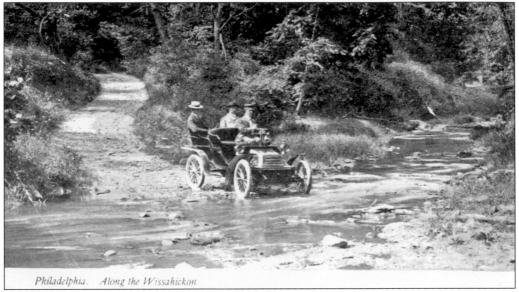

Philadelphia. Along the Wissahickon

In 1908, there was nothing stopping your chauffeur from driving your automobile along the Wissahickon Creek, except for the possibility of rough going such as at this ford, probably at the stream that meanders down beside Rex Avenue. This vehicle was made before 1905 by the Autocar Company in Ardmore and was steered by a crank, not a steering wheel. The Germantown and Chestnut Hill Improvement Association championed the protest against autos in the upper Wissahickon Valley in 1910 and again in the early 1920s, hence the name Forbidden Drive.

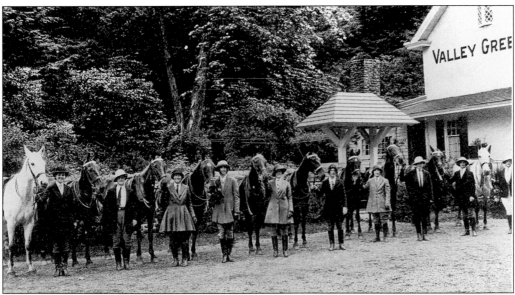

The Riders and Drivers Association was formed in 1912 to show the value of keeping the Wissahickon free of automobiles. Every spring since then, horses parade past the Valley Green Inn on Wissahickon Day. In 1927, these private school girls were photographed during one of their saddle horse club outings by the inn. Mills still lined the Wissahickon Creek in the 1850s, when the Valley Green Hotel was built for travelers and those who wished to enjoy the Wissahickon area.

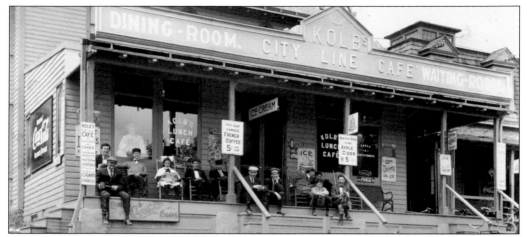

Kolb's, on Northwestern Avenue across the street from the northern end of Fairmount Park, was the place to go for oysters, cigars, and ice cream *c.* 1909. Next door to the right is Rolo's Restaurant, now Bruno's Restaurant. The Philadelphia Rapid Transit trolley made a loop to return south in front of these two buildings where there is a roadway today. Riders waited here to catch the trolley to Reading.

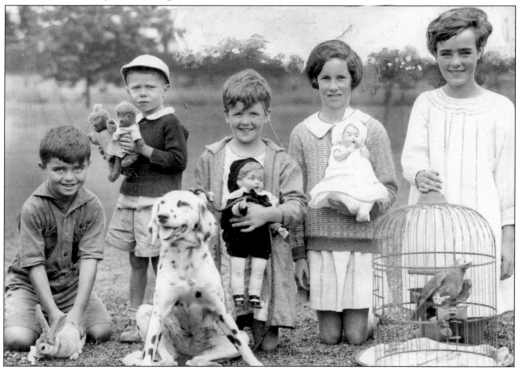

In 1910, George Woodward proposed that the Germantown and Chestnut Hill Improvement Association convert the abandoned waterworks land owned by the City of Philadelphia into a playground and recreation center. Many believed that although Chestnut Hill was on the edge of the country, most of the open land was in private hands and therefore children from modest homes were forced to play in the streets. The water tower was retained as a picturesque feature. Regina Quinn, of 8135 Ardleigh Street, did well at the Water Tower Pet and Doll Show in 1929, as her dog Dot won first prize, and her doll won third prize.

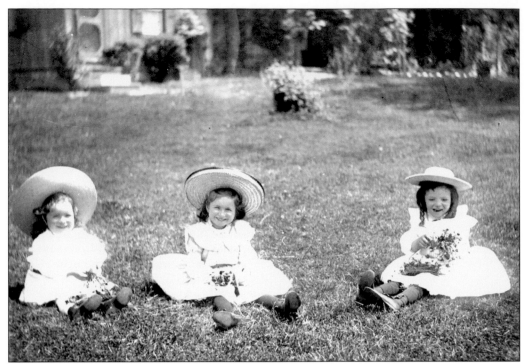

Wearing sunbonnets and holding flowers are, from left to right, Louise Boyer (born 1899), her sister Ethel (born 1896), and their cousin Gladys. Louise and Ethel grew up comfortably in Chestnut Hill. A few years after this photograph was taken, their father, Gabriel Boyer, who worked for the Reading Railroad, died suddenly of a heart attack at age 30. Their mother, Helena Grebe Boyer, was forced to take up work as a dressmaker and lived above McNaughton's Bakery on Bethlehem Pike. The family could not afford nearby Springside School, so Louise went to Germantown High School for two years and left when offered a job.

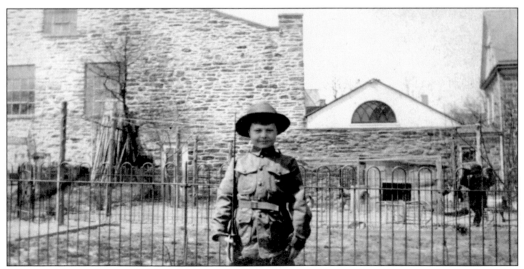

Clinton Moore (born 1907), in a miniature doughboy uniform, played army in his backyard at 7928 Germantown Avenue as World War I raged in Europe. Behind him is the former garage at 12 West Willow Grove Avenue.

Eight
MODERN CHESTNUT HILL

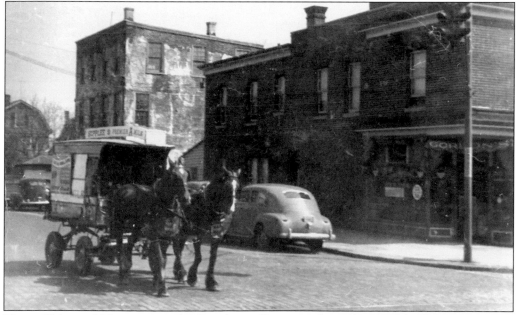

Horses Zeke and Harry power the Supplee milk wagon down East Highland Avenue in the mid-1940s, with 8441 Germantown Avenue in the background. The scene is evocative of the village-like atmosphere that prevailed in Chestnut Hill well after World War II. However, these years would bring massive change to the community in the form of higher taxes, the breakup of large estates, denser development, heavier traffic, and the growth of surrounding suburbs. After years of semi-rural isolation, Chestnut Hill was poised to plunge into the tumult of postwar Philadelphia.

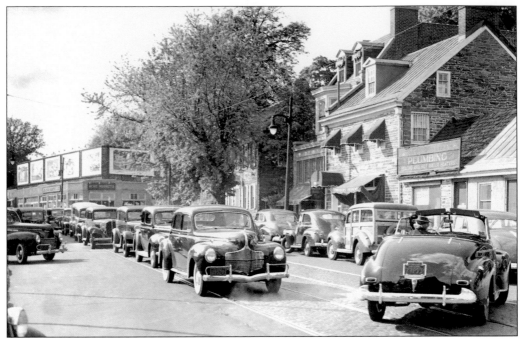

Traffic jams were already a problem in Chestnut Hill before America entered World War II, as this 1941 photograph indicates. With the proliferation of cars after the war, many Germantown Avenue shops sat vacant as people drove to the suburbs to shop. The building, with billboards in the background, is a shopping arcade that occupied the site of the Maple Shade Inn from 1927 until 1947, when it was replaced by a Gulf gas station.

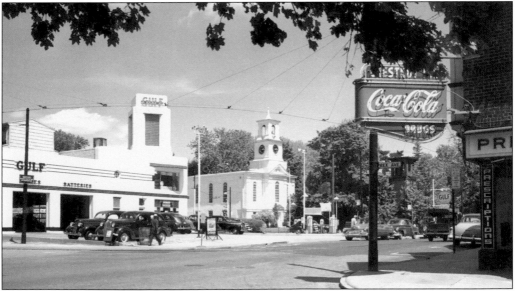

On March 6, 1947, the Gulf station at left welcomed its first customer, Elsie Douglas, who had her LaSalle filled with No-Nox. In the 1960s, the gleaming structure was replaced with a colonial structure deemed more appropriate to Chestnut Hill. Today, a Borders bookstore occupies the fork of the roads. The drugstore to the right is the Chestnut Hill Pharmacy, at 8640 Germantown Avenue (now Edward Jones Investments).

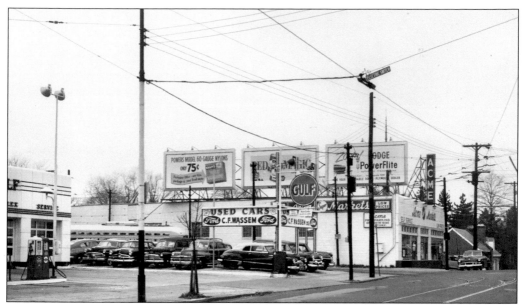

The Acme supermarket on Bethlehem Pike (above) and the Grove Diner on Germantown Avenue opposite Rex Avenue (below) illustrate the cluttered, unkempt atmosphere of Germantown Avenue after World War II, especially around the trolley loop behind the Gulf station. In the early 1970s, these buildings would be demolished and replaced by the Top of the Hill, a shopping plaza financed by the community-funded Chestnut Hill Realty Trust as part of a campaign to beautify and revitalize the commercial district. Today, Top of the Hill houses the Pendleton Store (on the Acme site), Roller's Restaurant and Market, and other stores and offices. In the 1960s, the Chestnut Hill Realty Trust also purchased a decrepit garage and car showroom on West Highland Avenue and turned it into the Highland West Mall, a block of shops and restaurants.

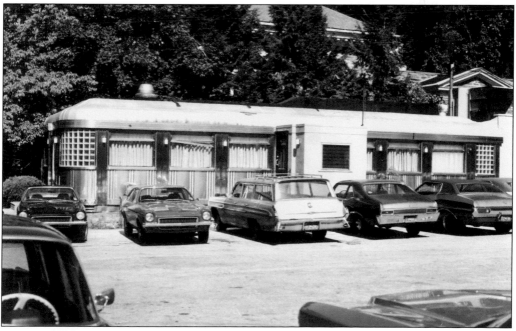

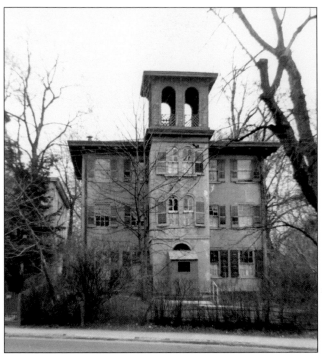

The Wharton Homestead, at 8623 Germantown Avenue (south of the Baptist church), was a Chestnut Hill landmark and home to the Wharton family for nearly a century. In 1956, it was torn down and replaced by a modern bank building for the Intercounty Savings & Loan Association. The destruction of this beautiful Italianate villa, a Federal house remodeled in 1840, helped alert Chestnut Hillers to their vanishing architectural heritage.

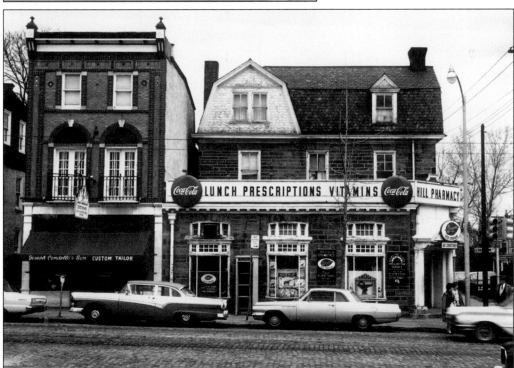

Many older buildings in Chestnut Hill's shopping district also fell victim to urban clutter. The Hill Pharmacy, shown here in the early 1960s, was located at 8401 Germantown Avenue, at the corner of Gravers Lane. It occupied the 19th-century residence of the Graver family, for whom Gravers Lane is named. Today, the building has been renovated and houses Manner & Knoll.

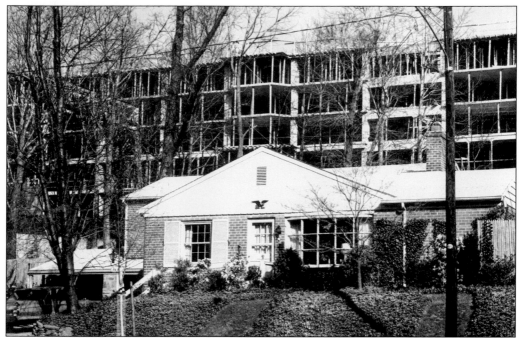

In 1963, construction began on Hill House on West Evergreen Avenue, one of two high-rise buildings in Chestnut Hill (along with Hilltower Apartments). The newly organized Land Use Planning Committee (LUPC) opposed the 11-story structure but was defeated in court. Although Hill House became a favorite address for elderly residents, community organization has helped to prevent the construction of other high-rise buildings, maintaining Chestnut Hill's low-rise profile.

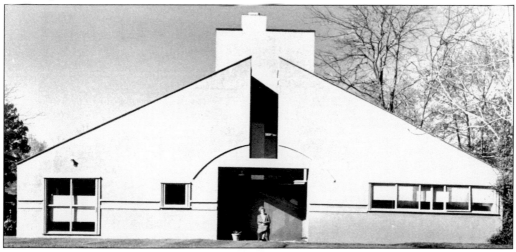

A few blocks from Hill House, a modern landmark took shape. In 1959, a young architect named Robert Venturi designed a small house for his widowed mother. Vanna Venturi (seen here after the house's completion in 1964) lived at 8330 Millman Street until shortly before her death in 1975. Today, Mother's House is considered a masterpiece of innovative design. Venturi, Scott Brown, & Associates (VSBA), the Philadelphia firm founded by Venturi and wife Denise Scott Brown, is an international leader in architectural design. (Photograph by Rollin R. LaFrance.)

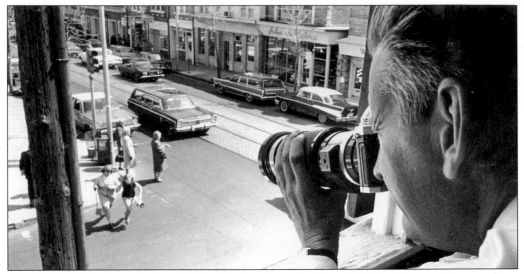

From the 1940s through the 1970s, St. Louis native Lloyd Wells (shown photographing Germantown Avenue in the early 1960s) was a leader in changing Chestnut Hill by revitalizing its commercial district and creating local quasi governmental bodies. Wells helped to found or reorganize the Chestnut Hill Development Group (predecessor to the Business Association), the Chestnut Hill Parking Association, the Chestnut Hill Realty Trust, the *Chestnut Hill Local*, and the Chestnut Hill Community Association.

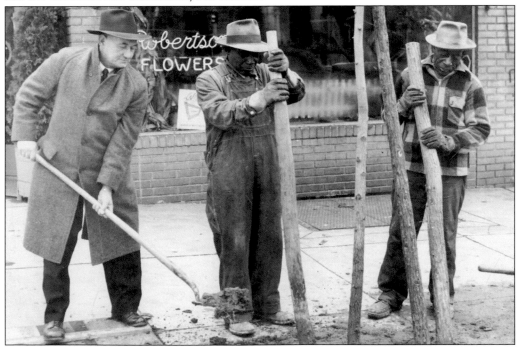

In the early 1950s, about 30 percent of the stores on Germantown Avenue were vacant. One of Wells' first steps in revitalizing the business district was to "green" Germantown Avenue, convincing merchants to have ginkgo trees planted in front of their stores for $33.50 per tree. Here, Chestnut Hill Development Group workers plant a tree before Robertson Florists, then located at 8339 Germantown Avenue.

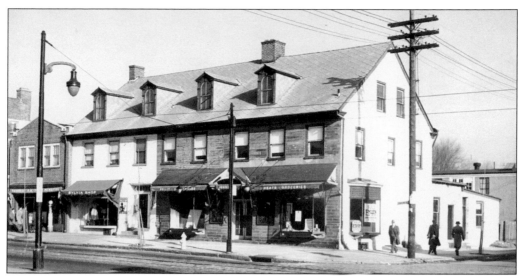

Envisioning Germantown Avenue as a horizontal department store, Wells and the Chestnut Hill Development Group (CHDG) convinced merchants to remove neon signs and renovate their façades in a homogenous colonial style. The former Cress's Hotel at Germantown and Highland Avenues (see page 13), shown above in the early 1950s, was one of the first buildings to be "colonialized." A grocery store before its remodeling, it became the new home of Robertson Florists, still located there. When the building opened in 1952, thousands jammed Germantown Avenue to see it, and nearly 2,000 corsages were given out. The colonialization of Germantown Avenue was deemed complete with the remodeling of the former Miss Huston's department store at 8618–8620 Germantown Avenue (seen below) in 1961 (now the Citizens/Mellon Bank building). Chestnut Hill celebrated with a parade on April 20, 1961, with marchers attired in colonial costumes.

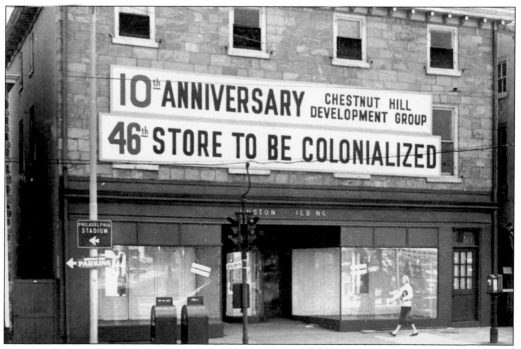

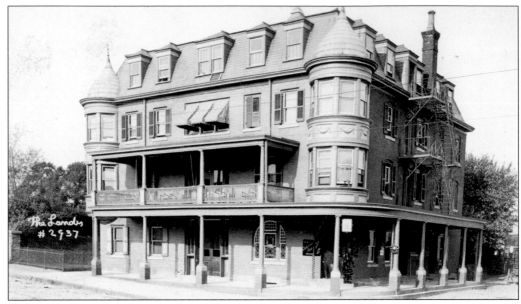

Colonialization worked less well on Victorian structures. The exuberant and eclectic Chestnut Hill Hotel opened in 1894 at 8229 Germantown Avenue. During Prohibition, it degenerated into a speakeasy and, according to some local residents, a bordello. In 1957–1958, the hotel had its turrets and porches removed and was remodeled into a featureless bulk with a pseudo-colonial entrance. In the early 1980s, it was renovated again, becoming the core of a retail complex named the Centre of Chestnut Hill. A wing was added on its Southampton Avenue side that now houses the Melting Pot and Stella Notte restaurants. The hotel's carriage house and stables became stores and a farmers' market.

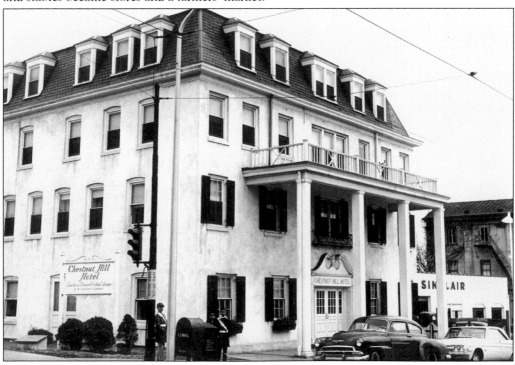

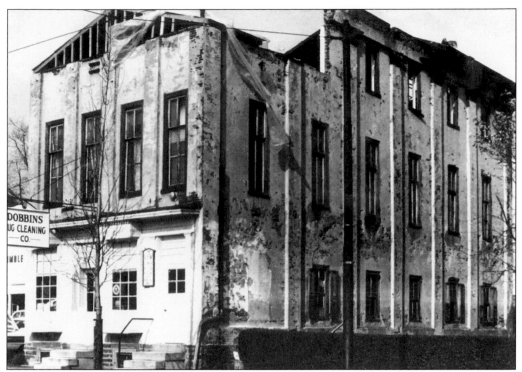

The threatened demolition of the 1859 Hiram Lodge building at 8217–19 Germantown Avenue in 1966 (above) led to the formation of the Chestnut Hill Historical Society (CHHS) by Ann Spaeth, Nancy Hubby, Shirley Hanson, and other concerned residents. Since its founding, CHHS volunteers and employees have rescued other historic buildings, written an architectural history of the community, established Chestnut Hill as a historic district on the National Register of Historic Places, and developed a highly successful conservation and façade easement program to preserve notable structures and open spaces. The 1980 photograph below shows founding members Nancy Hubby and Shirley Hanson in front of 8810 Norwood Avenue, one of three Victorian houses slated for demolition by Chestnut Hill Hospital. Although 8810 eventually fell to the wrecker's ball, CHHS was able to preserve and restore the other two.

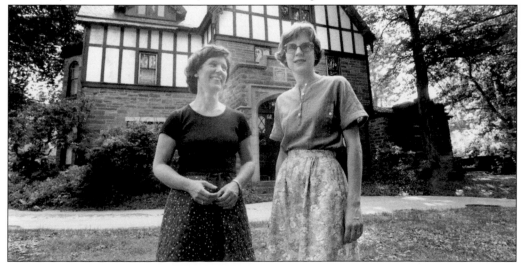

The Chestnut Hill Local

VOL. 1 – No. 2   8419 GERMANTOWN AVENUE, PHILADELPHIA, PA., THURSDAY, MAY 22, 1958   CHestnut Hill 8-4250

Huge Meeting Decides Fate of Morgan Tract

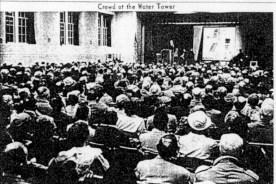

Crowd at the Water Tower

Community Accepts Committee's Proposals

Nearly eight hundred residents and citizens of Chestnut Hill and its environs turned out for the Community Association meeting on the Morgan Tract Committee report on May 6th.

Mr. J. Pennington Straus, president of the Community Association opened the meeting. He praised the large turnout and reviewed the history of the Morgan Tract. He recalled the fact that the Morgan family had sold the 90 acre estate to Temple University for a new campus, that Myer Blum, a Philadelphia developer, acquired an option from Temple. Because Mr. Blum failed to accumulate the necessary financial resources, he did not take up his option. Temple then sold the land to the Summit Construction Co. of New York in June of 1956.

Mr. Straus then called on Mr. John Bodine, Chairman of the Morgan Tract Committee. Mr. Bodine, with deliberate care and thought recounted the negotiations the committee has had with the Summit Co. over several years. He told of the developer's hope for high rise apartments, and a 100,000 square foot shopping center located on Stenton Ave. and Willow Grove. He expressed the neighbor's and community's hope for keeping the status quo - another estate or green park or several fine houses. He told of the pressures of the city for tax revenue on one hand the owners' desire for reasonable profit on the other.

Mr. Bodine then outlined the compromise agreement which the committee would make with the construction company, if the Community Association approved. The Summit Company asked for a zoning change from A to H-2, and agreed: to put the shopping center on Willow Grove Ave. next to the Wyndmoor railroad station, limiting its size to 75,000 square feet; to make planting strips around parking spaces; to limit dwelling units to 1200, covering not more than thirty-five percent of the ground area; the dog leg of the tract to be single houses; sign covenants limiting the size of the development for twenty-five years.

After some factual questions from the floor, Mr. Bodine read a resolution moving the adoption of the committee's recommendations.

Several community leaders spoke on behalf of civic groups.

Mr. Jesse Nalle, chairman of the Land Planning Committee of Chestnut Hill Community Association, reported that his committee voted unanimously to support the Morgan Tract Committee as the best long term land use pattern for the good of the community.

Mr. George Pilling, president of the Chestnut Hill Community Center, spoke in unanimous support of the agreement.

Mr. Thomas Ryan, president of the Chestnut Hill-Mt. Airy Businessmen's Association, pledged

(Cont'd. on p. 5)

Broad Street Trust Remodels Post Office

by HENRY CADWALADER

The Broad Street Trust Company has spared no pains to make the Chestnut Hill Post Office as up to date and as useful as possible. The bank owns the building, and leases it to the government. Lack of space in the Chestnut Hill Post Office building induced the bank, lessors of the building, to make many changes and improvements. Mr. Russell Fenner, President of the Chestnut Hill Branch of the Broad Street Trust Company, says that the work is now practically completed.

The major changes which produced the required space were, moving the leading platform to the outside of the building, and providing a new "swing room" or rest room for mailmen in the basement.

These alterations permitted the use of the entire ground floor space for the sorting and handling of mail, as well as for the installation of an attractive lobby.

In line with Chestnut Hill redevelopment ideas, the colonial theme was enhanced by the addition of wrought iron railings at the entrances. Modern fluorescent lighting fixtures have been installed throughout, and the entire building is now air-conditioned. Tile wainscoting adds to the cheerful modern atmosphere which is complemented by the brand new counters and post office box supplied by the United States Government.

Chestnut Hill residents can take pride in their fine new post office, and the Broad Street Trust Company is to be congratulated on the tasteful manner in which it has modernized this vital unit to the community.

Good Music Near

On Thursday, May 22 and Friday, May 23, at 8:00 p.m., the choir, soloists and orchestra of the Unitarian Church of Germantown will present two different programs of representative works of Mozart, with the Requiem as the final number on Friday night. In addition, Joseph D. Chapline, Jr., the musical director, has assembled a brass choir, which will play compositions by Gabrieli and Hendrick Andriesen. The soloists are Beth Oughton, Soprano, Joyce Lundy, Contralto, William H. Parsons, Tenor, and Robert Solly, Bass, with Edgar D. Ebenbach at the organ. There will be no admission charge, and parking space is available behind the church.

These programs are intended to bring to performance great choral and instrumental music, but their primary purpose is to provide opportunity for as many people as possible to come together and enjoy a spirit of community while they work together as performers and as listeners to learn about Mozart.

Local Robbery

Thomas J. Walsh, president of the Chestnut Hill-Mt. Airy Businessmen's Association and assistant secretary of the Broad Street Trust Company was robbed on May 13th at his home at 7505 Germantown Ave. Taken was one hundred dollars in cash and a hundred dollars worth of jewelry. The theft occurred between ten and twelve a. m. Access was gained by a cellar window. Police have been notified.

Glee Clubs To Present King David

On Friday, May 23rd at 8:15, in the new Springside auditorium the combined Chestnut Hill Academy, Springside Glee Clubs will present Honegger's "King David". Co-conductors for the performance are Lisa Fredericks and Albert Conkey. Julia Heide and Thomas Farry, soprano and tenor soloists from the Chestnut Hill Presbyterian Church, will sing the solo parts with Albert Nesbitt, CHA '58, as the narrator.

Students from the two schools who will play in the orchestral ensemble for the performance are: Frederic Ballard, Sophie Ballard, Tom Fernley, Jack Beecham, William Edwards and David Parachini.

Springside Glee Club officers are: Elizabeth Sturges, '58, president, Elizabeth Frey, '58, librarian, and Anne Lingelbach, accompanist.

Chestnut Hill Academy officers are: William McCook, '58, president, Clarence Wurts, secretary-treasurer, and Frederic Ballard and John Tuton, librarians.

Springside To Be Dedicated

Invitations have been issued by the Board of Directors of Springside School for the Dedication Service of the new school on June 11 - at 5:15 p.m.

Speaker at the service will be Mrs. Samuel H. Paul, assistant to the President of Bryn Mawr College, and former Headmistress of Springside.

Jenks Concert

The Jenks School Elementary Glee Club presented its Spring Concert on Thursday, May 8th in the school auditorium, Miss Ethel Stalker conducted.

Plans Formulated For Human Resources

The Chestnut Hill Community today possesses an untouched gold mine of available human resources. Many segments of our society for various reasons find themselves out of a job. These people fall into three general classifications, the largest of which are the retired older citizens. The second group are those who are qualified for normal gainful employment, but who, for one reason or another, have been unable to get a specific job. The smallest group comprises those individuals who have had the misfortune of experiencing a major accident and who, having recuperated from a period of hospitalization, find themselves unable to assume the role of their previous life. All of these groups of people constitute a resource of valuable service which is being wasted.

Realizing this problem, the Chestnut Hill Development Group is endeavoring to organize a Human Resources Agency whose goal it will be to classify these individuals on the one hand, and to seek on the other, to find a suitable outlet for the individual's capabilities.

These outlets or jobs can be either voluntary or financially remunerative as both situations provide a valuable outlet for the ability of the particular individual.

For example, many of the retired men do not need financial remuneration, but do need the stimulating intellectual challenge of a regular interest, without which their lives in the most part become meaningless.

The service which the Chestnut Hill Development Group hopes to render through this activity can be invaluable not only to the individuals themselves, but to the institutions who are needful of these human resources.

Although the Development Group has operated a small and limited service of this nature, the increasing demand for this service today requires help beyond the budget limitations of the organization.

If any reader is interested in working in this field on a volunteer basis, we hope he will get in touch with the Chestnut Hill Development Group, 5419 Germantown Avenue

---

In the early 1950s, the Randal Morgan estate (see page 65) was sold to a developer who planned to erect six high-rise apartment buildings and a large shopping complex. Community leaders reorganized the Chestnut Hill Community Association to negotiate with the builder, reaching a compromise where a lower-density development with only one high-rise was built. The *Chestnut Hill Local*—the third issue of which, dated May 22, 1958, is shown here—was founded during this period to keep residents aware of the Morgan Tract controversy and other local issues. Today, the *Local* is a prize-winning community newspaper. The Community Association, with 33 committees and 2,500 household members, helps to shape community policy on all key local issues.

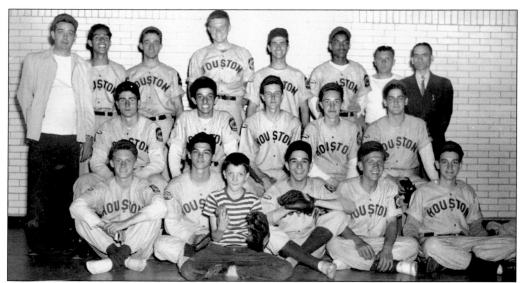

After World War II, Chestnut Hill struggled with integration and civil rights. Rudy Miles, whose mother Bessie appears on page 53, was the only African-American teenager on the baseball team, which was sponsored by the Henry H. Houston 2nd Post No. 3 of the American Legion. The 1948 photograph (above) shows him at the Water Tower Recreation Center, next to director Mike Giantisco (third and second from right, top row). Although some Legionnaires did not want Rudy on the team, Giantisco demanded that he participate. Rudy went on to become a star collegiate athlete, a minor league baseball player, and a Philadelphia teacher before retiring to Chestnut Hill. The photograph below shows participants in a 1967 seminar entitled "Black Power—White Power," cosponsored by Chestnut Hill and Germantown churches. While Chestnut Hill remained segregated longer than much of Philadelphia, its African-American population increased from 1 percent in 1970 to 15 percent in 2000.

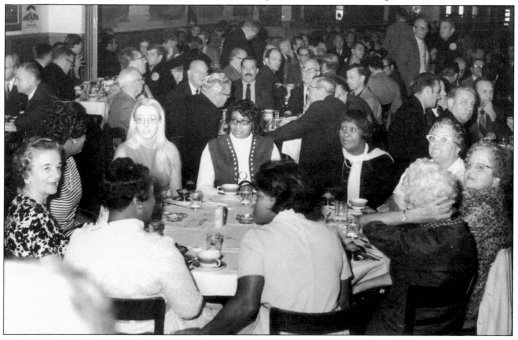

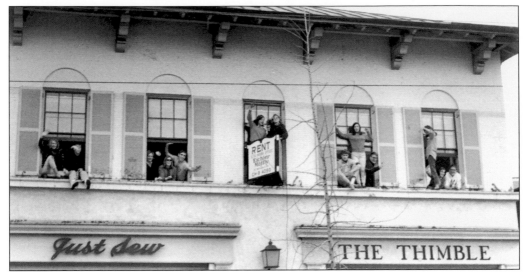

In February 1966, local teenagers working with the Community Association opened the Orange Ell youth center in the upper floor of 8434 Germantown Avenue, organizing dances, a coffee house, poetry readings, plays, and other activities. Among the celebrants above are Susan Miller, Pam Warwick, Marnie Vail, Willie Longstreth, Ricky Rothstein, Halsy North, and Joe Woolston. After the Orange Ell closed in 1968, the Community Association and *Chestnut Hill Local* moved into the location.

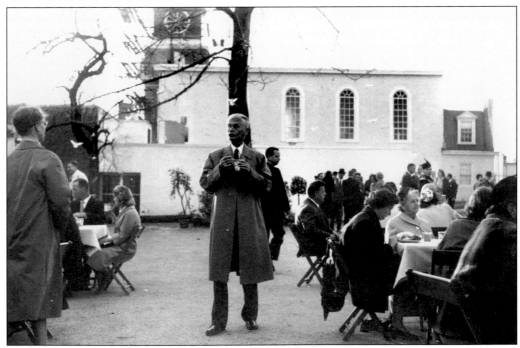

The Chestnut Hill Parking Foundation was founded in 1953 to develop off-street parking lots and offer shoppers an alternative to suburban malls. This 1954 photograph shows George Woodward Jr. at the party to open the first lot, in the 8600 block of Germantown Avenue. In its first year, the Parking Foundation handled 34,000 cars. Today, it operates nine lots that accommodate more than 600,000 cars per year.

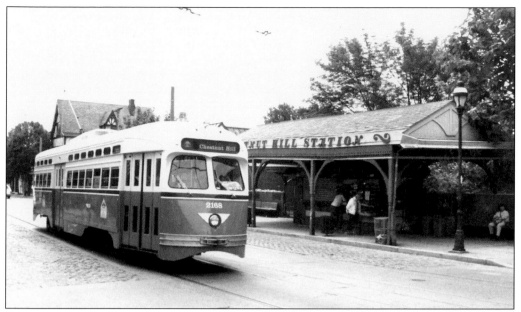

For a century, the Route 23 electric trolley extended from 11th and Bigler Streets in South Philadelphia to Germantown Avenue and Bethlehem Pike. In 1992, budgetary pressures forced SEPTA to limit service to the weekends, when restored trolleys like this one replaced buses on Germantown Avenue. In June 1996, SEPTA suspended trolley service completely, except for special events. Germantown Avenue remains a dedicated trolley route, keeping alive the possibility that the trolleys may return.

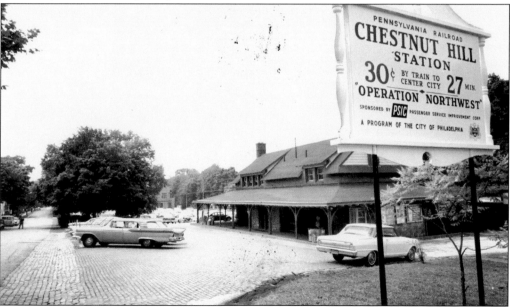

While Chestnut Hill continued to be a railroad suburb, the decline of the Reading and Pennsylvania Railroads in the 1960s, followed by SEPTA's budgetary restraints, caused service disruptions and the deterioration of local train stations. The Chestnut Hill West station (shown here in 1965) was renovated in the 1990s as a branch of Chestnut Hill National Bank. Various volunteer groups have stepped in to repair and maintain other stations.

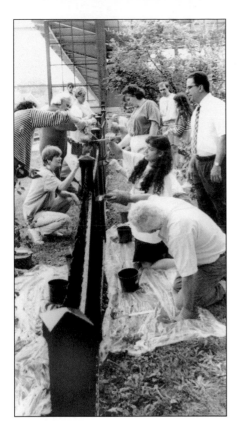

In May 1996, Chestnut Hill Historical Society volunteers (including then-director Howard Kittell in the right background) painted fences and planted flowers at the Chestnut Hill East station. The society also restored the historic Frank Furness Gravers Lane station in the 1980s (see page 23). As in the past, Chestnut Hill's volunteer groups play a vital role in bridging the gap between the community's needs and increasingly limited municipal services. (Photograph by Joe Morsello.)

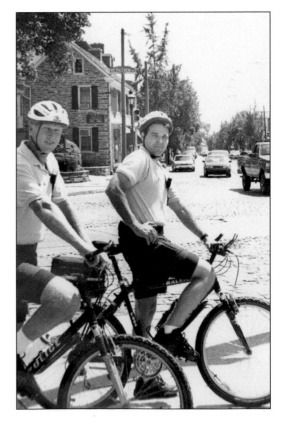

Philadelphia crime rates soared in the 1980s, prompting the formation of town watch groups in Chestnut Hill. Local residents were concerned over the time it took police at Germantown's 14th Precinct to respond to crimes in the Hill. After much protest, two bicycle patrolmen were assigned to Chestnut Hill in May 1994. This 2000 photograph by Joe Morsello shows patrolmen Rich Paraschak and Joe Bird at the top of the Hill.

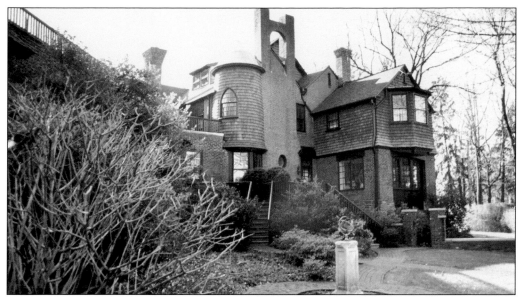

Many historic structures have been adapted for other uses. In 1983, Richard Snowden purchased Anglecot at Prospect and Evergreen Avenues and converted the historic Wilson Eyre structure to condominiums. In 1980, Druim Moir (see page 72) was adapted into multiple residential units by Sallie Smith Kise, great-granddaughter of Henry H. Houston, and her husband, architect James N. Kise. The Woodward family continues the conversion of Krisheim (see page 79) from institutional to residential use.

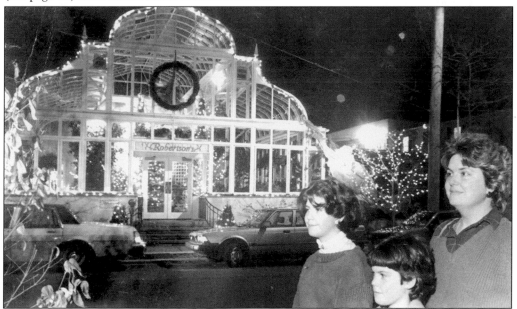

Faced with competition from suburban malls and nearby neighborhoods such as Manayunk, Chestnut Hill works hard to attract visitors and shoppers with unique shops and colorful spring and autumn festivals. In 1986, Robertson Florists opened a Victorian glass-and-iron conservatory on East Highland Avenue, featuring fountains, statuary, and colorful tiles. Vivian Maginnis and her daughters Jennifer and Beth visit Stag & Doe nights, Chestnut Hill's annual nighttime Christmas event, pass by the sparkling conservatory.

127

PHOTOGRAPH CREDITS

Athenaeum of Philadelphia (Bruce Laverty): 12b
Atwater Kent Museum (Jeffrey Ray and Susan Drinan): 22t, 111t
Justin M. and Nancy Dunning Baxter: 25b
David Bower: 19b, 36b, 107b, 110t
Will Brown: 125t
Chestnut Hill Academy: 70t, 90t/b
Chestnut Hill Local (Katie Worrall): 89t, 92t, 115t, 116t, 117t, 126t/b, 127b
The Dwyer family: 48t/b, 95t
Free Library of Philadelphia (Joseph Benford): 60t
Germantown Historical Society: 10t, 11b, 13t, 14b, 16t, 18t/b, 19t, 20t/b, 22b, 43t, 49b, 83b, 84, 99b, 105t/b, 107t
Hugh Gilmore: 50t, 82b, 87t, 96t
Russell Goudy Jr.: 46t
Historical Society of Pennsylvania (HSP), Campbell Collection (Jordan Rockford): 13b, 15t/b, 106b
Raymond Holstein: 26b
Sarah Melcher Jarvis and Deborah Melcher Stout: 70b
Library Company of Philadelphia (Jenny Ambroise and Valerie Miller): 24t, 29b, 56, 67t, 106t, 108t/b, 109t
Library of Congress (Kennith Johnson): 11t, 66b
Hugh and Anne McNally: 54b
David Moore: 112b
Morris Arboretum of the University of Pennsylvania (Robert Gutowski): 66t
Philadelphia City Archives (Ward Childs): 35t/b, 76b
Philadelphia Water Department: 44t
St. Martin-in-the-Fields Episcopal Church (The Very Reverend Robert L. Tate): 69b, 73b, 87b
Gerry M. Serianni: 52t/b
Sallie L. O. Smith: 72t/b, 77b
Richard Wood Snowden: 61t/b
Springside School: 91t/b
Linda Stanley: 75t/b
Joseph C. Thomas Jr.: 42t/b
Urban Archives, Temple University Libraries (Evan Tolle): 45b, 97t, 103t, 111b, 114t, 120b, 121b, 125b
Venturi, Scott Brown, & Associates Inc. (Helene Weiss): 117b
Willet Stained Glass Studios Inc.: 81t/b
Woodmere Art Museum (Patricia H. Hoffman): 64b, 98t
Thomas Woodruff: 40b
Charles Woodward: 79t/b, 80t
Ted Xaras: 31t, 32t

(t = top of page; b = bottom of page.)